RUNAWAYS

DEAD WRONG

WRITER: **TERRY MOORE**
PENCILS: **HUMBERTO RAMOS**
INKS: **DAVE MEIKIS**
COLORS: **CHRISTINA STRAIN**
LETTERS: **VC'S JOE CARAMAGNA**
WITH **CORY PETIT**
ASSISTANT EDITOR: **DANIEL KETCHUM**
EDITOR: **NICK LOWE**

RUNAWAYS CREATED BY **BRIAN K. VAUGHAN** &
ADRIAN ALPHONA

COLLECTION EDITOR: **JENNIFER GRÜNWALD**
ASSISTANT EDITORS: **ALEX STARBUCK** & **JOHN DENNING**
EDITOR, SPECIAL PROJECTS: **MARK D. BEAZLEY**
SENIOR EDITOR, SPECIAL PROJECTS: **JEFF YOUNGQUIST**
SENIOR VICE PRESIDENT OF SALES: **DAVID GABRIEL**
BOOK DESIGNER: **RODOLFO MURAGUCHI**

EDITOR IN CHIEF: **JOE QUESADA**
PUBLISHER: **DAN BUCKLEY**
EXECUTIVE PRODUCER: **ALAN FINE**

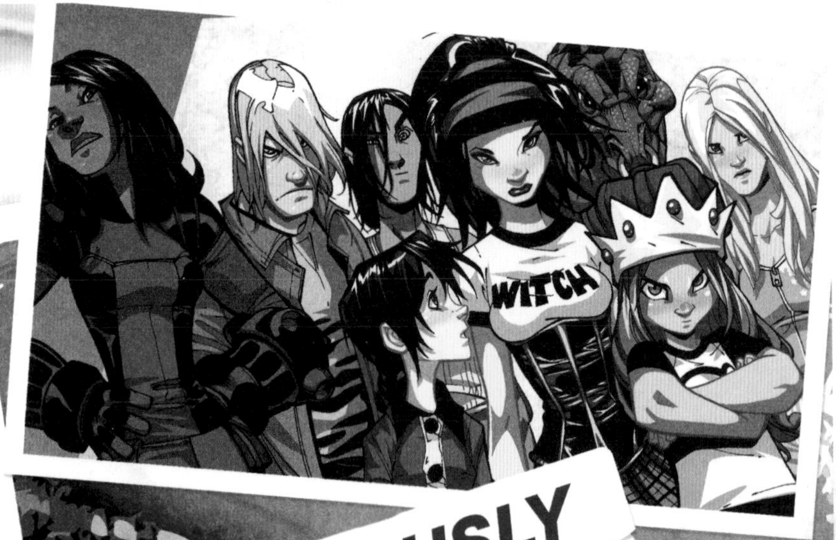
WITCH

PREVIOUSLY

AT SOME POINT IN THEIR LIVES, ALL KIDS THINK THAT THEIR PARENTS ARE EVIL. FOR MOLLY HAYES AND HER FRIENDS, THIS IS ESPECIALLY TRUE.

ONE NIGHT, MOLLY AND HER FRIENDS DISCOVERED THAT THEIR PARENTS WERE A GROUP OF SUPER-POWERED CRIME BOSSES WHO CALLED THEMSELVES "THE PRIDE." USING TECHNOLOGY AND RESOURCES STOLEN FROM THEIR PARENTS, THE TEENAGERS WERE ABLE TO STOP THE PRIDE AND BREAK THEIR CRIMINAL HOLD ON LOS ANGELES. BUT THEY'VE BEEN ON THE RUN ON EVER SINCE.

NOW, AFTER A FEW PERILOUS ADVENTURES IN NEW YORK CITY, NICO MINORU, CHASE STEIN, KAROLINA DEAN, MOLLY HAYES, VICTOR MANCHA, XAVIN AND KLARA ARE RETURNING TO THE CITY THEY KNOW BEST...

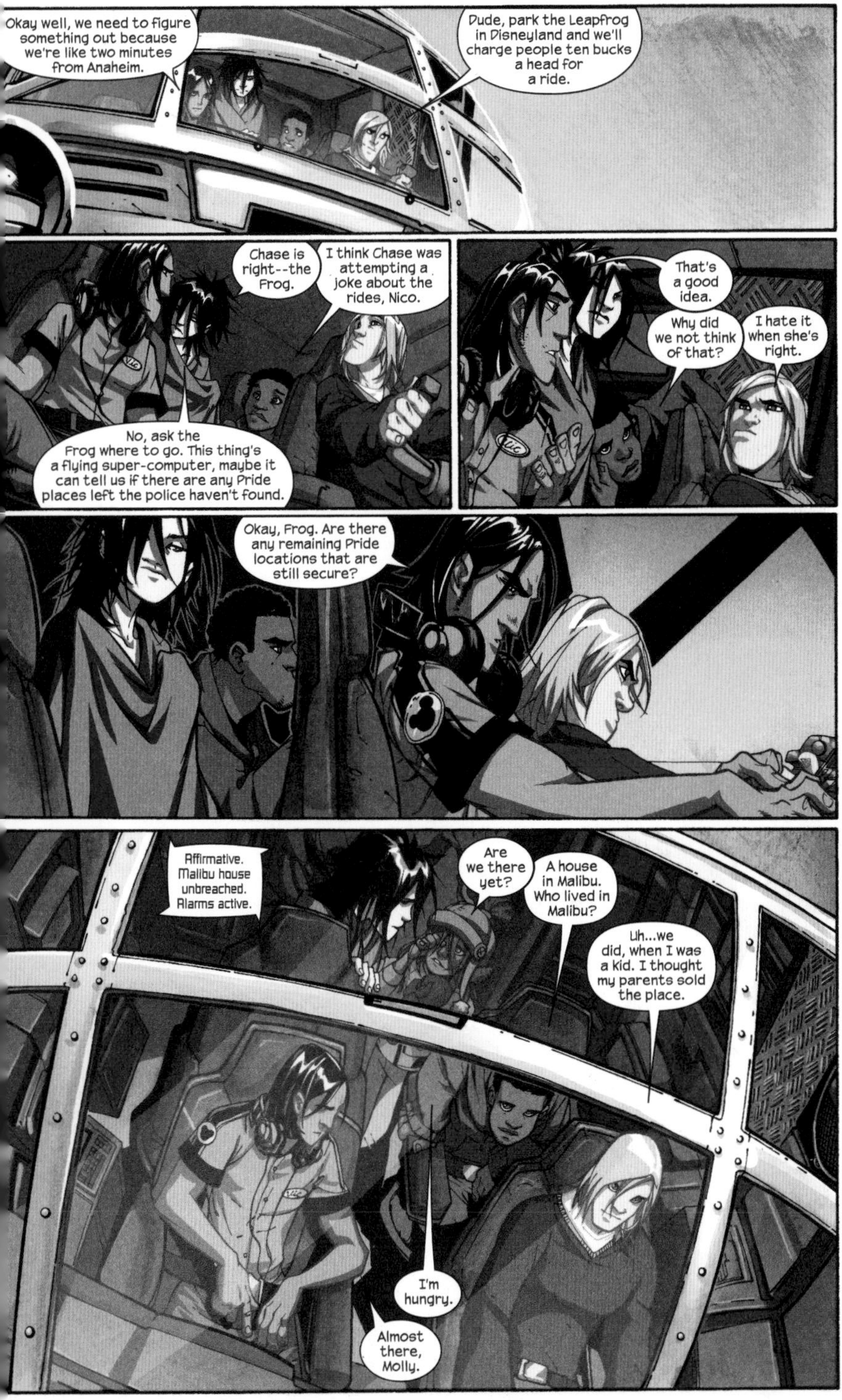
Okay well, we need to figure something out because we're like two minutes from Anaheim.
Dude, park the Leapfrog in Disneyland and we'll charge people ten bucks a head for a ride.
Chase is right--the Frog.
I think Chase was attempting a joke about the rides, Nico.
No, ask the Frog where to go. This thing's a flying super-computer, maybe it can tell us if there are any Pride places left the police haven't found.
That's a good idea.
Why did we not think of that?
I hate it when she's right.
Okay, Frog. Are there any remaining Pride locations that are still secure?
Affirmative. Malibu house unbreached. Alarms active.
Are we there yet?
A house in Malibu. Who lived in Malibu?
Uh...we did, when I was a kid. I thought my parents sold the place.
I'm hungry.
Almost there, Molly.

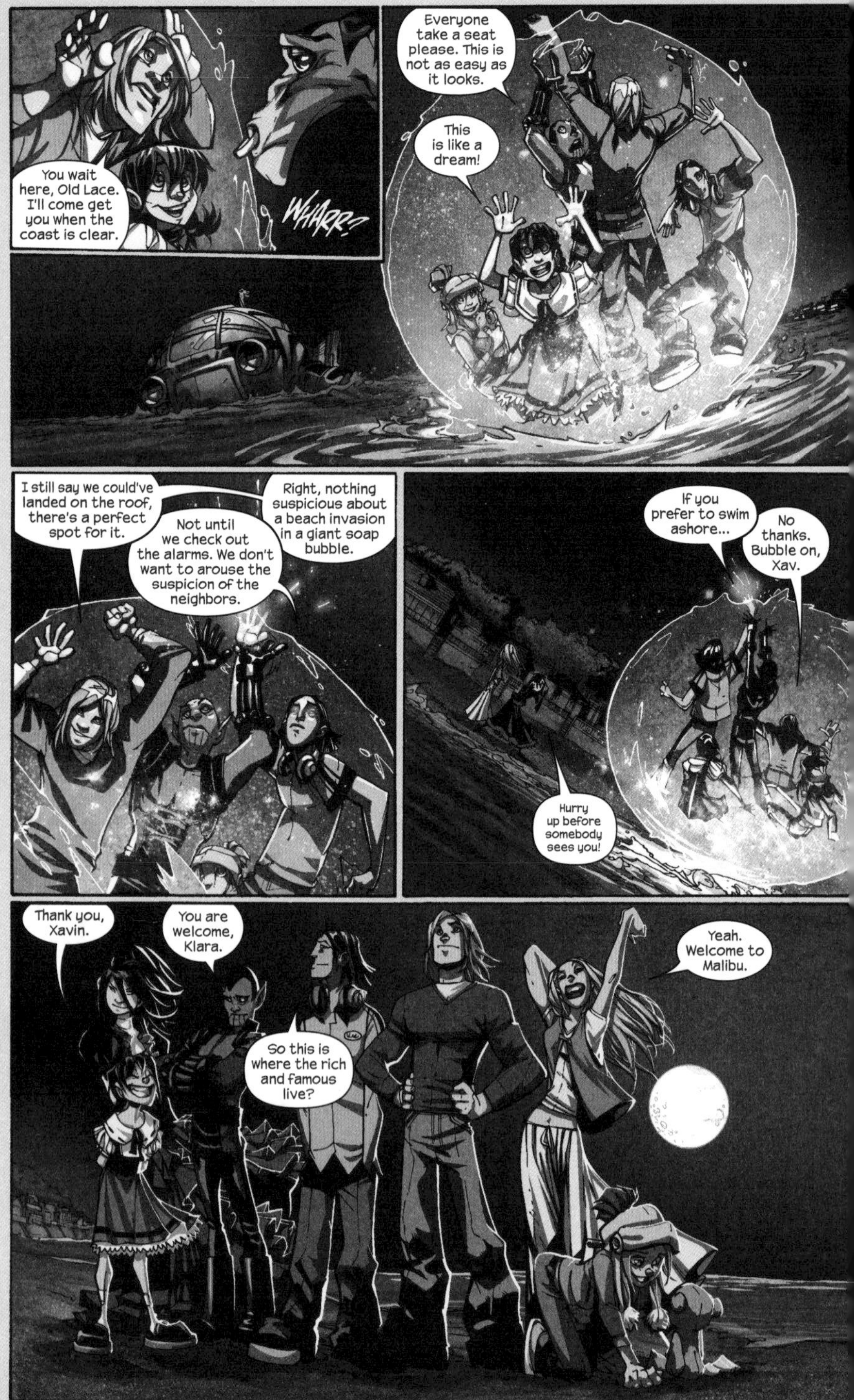

You wait here, Old Lace. I'll come get you when the coast is clear.
WHARR?
Everyone take a seat please. This is not as easy as it looks.
This is like a dream!
I still say we could've landed on the roof, there's a perfect spot for it.
Right, nothing suspicious about a beach invasion in a giant soap bubble.
Not until we check out the alarms. We don't want to arouse the suspicion of the neighbors.
If you prefer to swim ashore...
No thanks. Bubble on, Xav.
Hurry up before somebody sees you!
Thank you, Xavin.
You are welcome, Klara.
So this is where the rich and famous live?
Yeah. Welcome to Malibu.

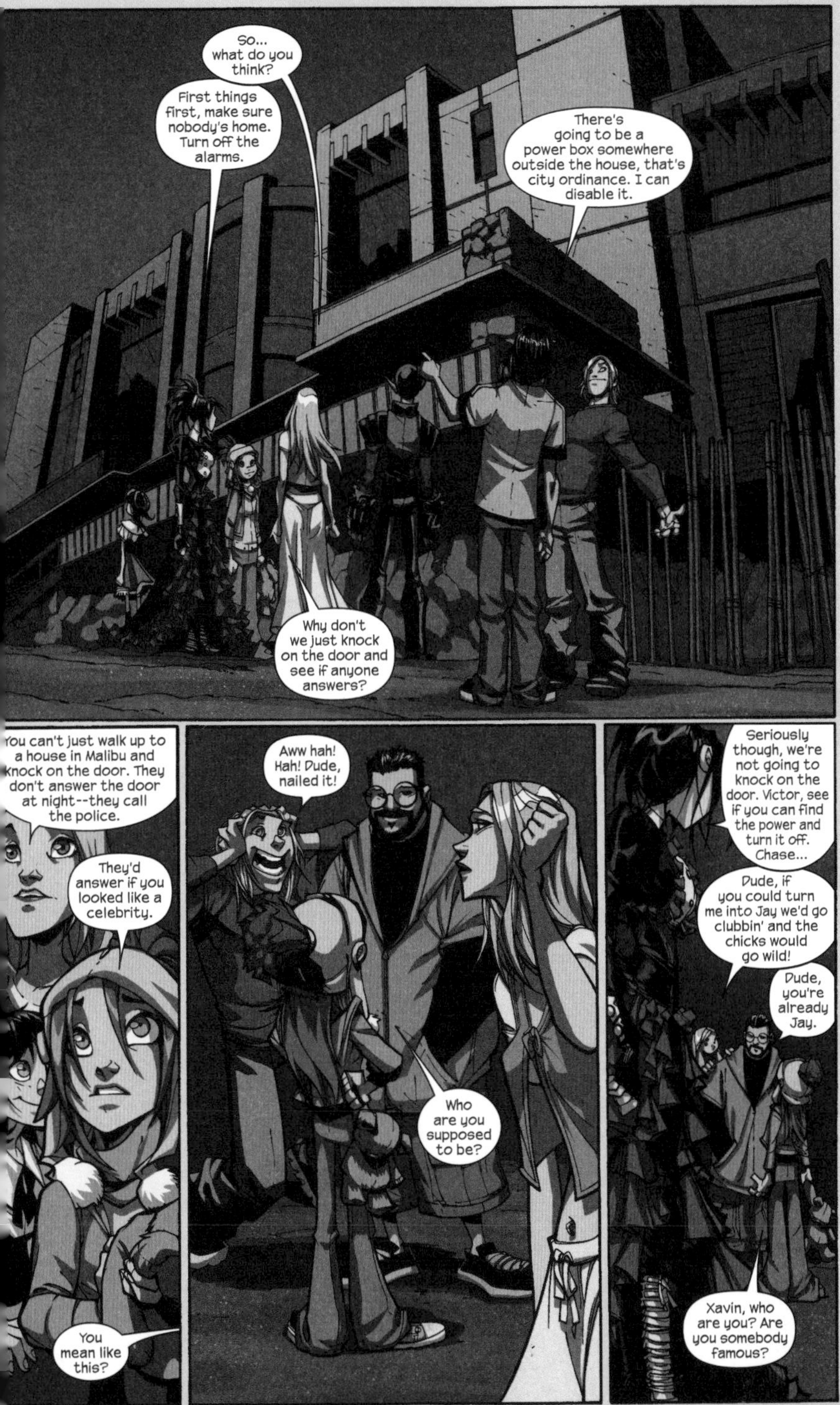
So... what do you think?
First things first, make sure nobody's home. Turn off the alarms.
There's going to be a power box somewhere outside the house, that's city ordinance. I can disable it.
Why don't we just knock on the door and see if anyone answers?
You can't just walk up to a house in Malibu and knock on the door. They don't answer the door at night--they call the police.
They'd answer if you looked like a celebrity.
You mean like this?
Aww hah! Hah! Dude, nailed it!
Who are you supposed to be?
Seriously though, we're not going to knock on the door. Victor, see if you can find the power and turn it off. Chase...
Dude, if you could turn me into Jay we'd go clubbin' and the chicks would go wild!
Dude, you're already Jay.
Xavin, who are you? Are you somebody famous?

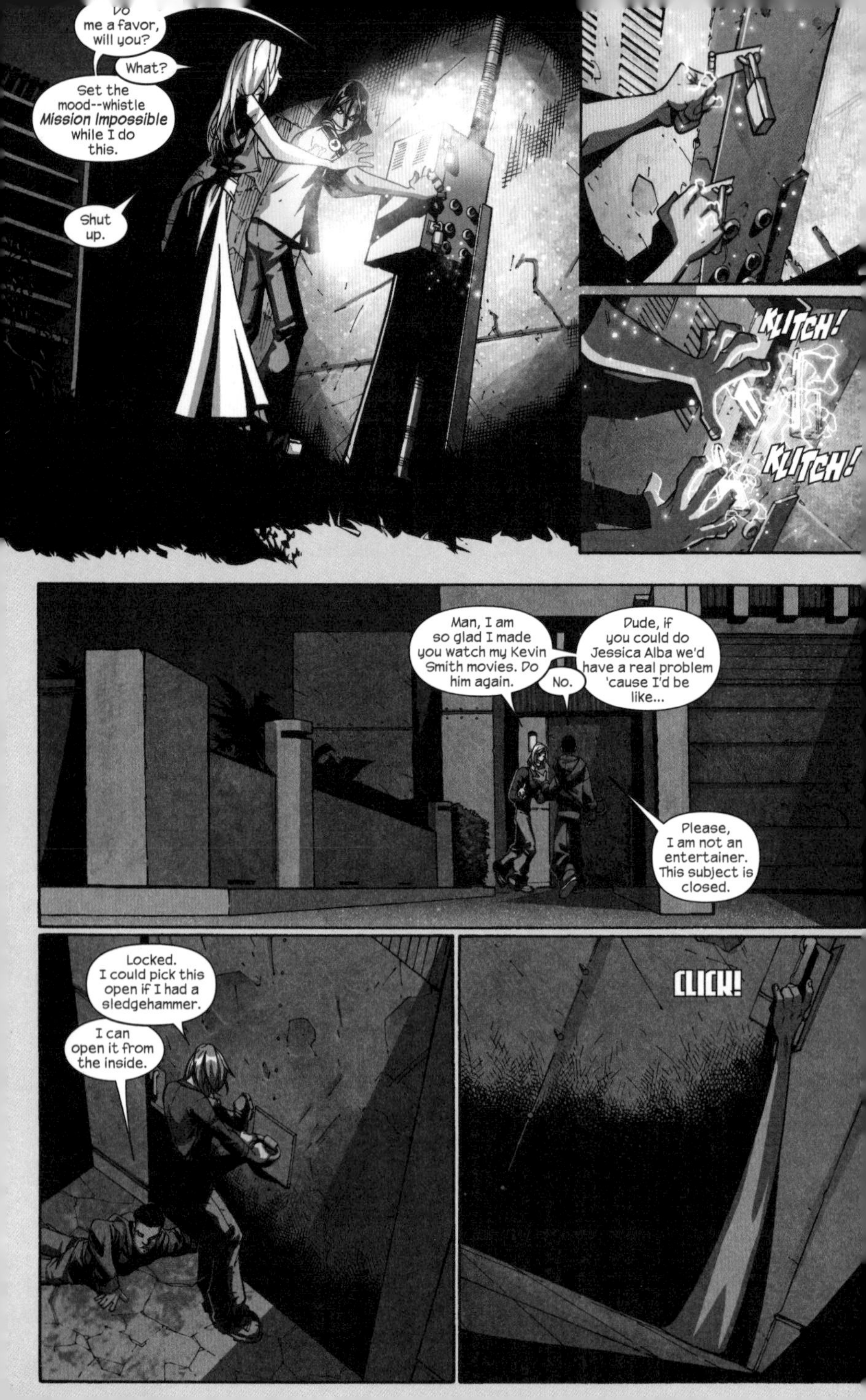
Do me a favor, will you?
What?
Set the mood--whistle *Mission Impossible* while I do this.
Shut up.
KLITCH!
KLITCH!
Man, I am so glad I made you watch my Kevin Smith movies. Do him again.
No.
Dude, if you could do Jessica Alba we'd have a real problem 'cause I'd be like...
Please, I am not an entertainer. This subject is closed.
Locked. I could pick this open if I had a sledgehammer.
I can open it from the inside.
CLICK!

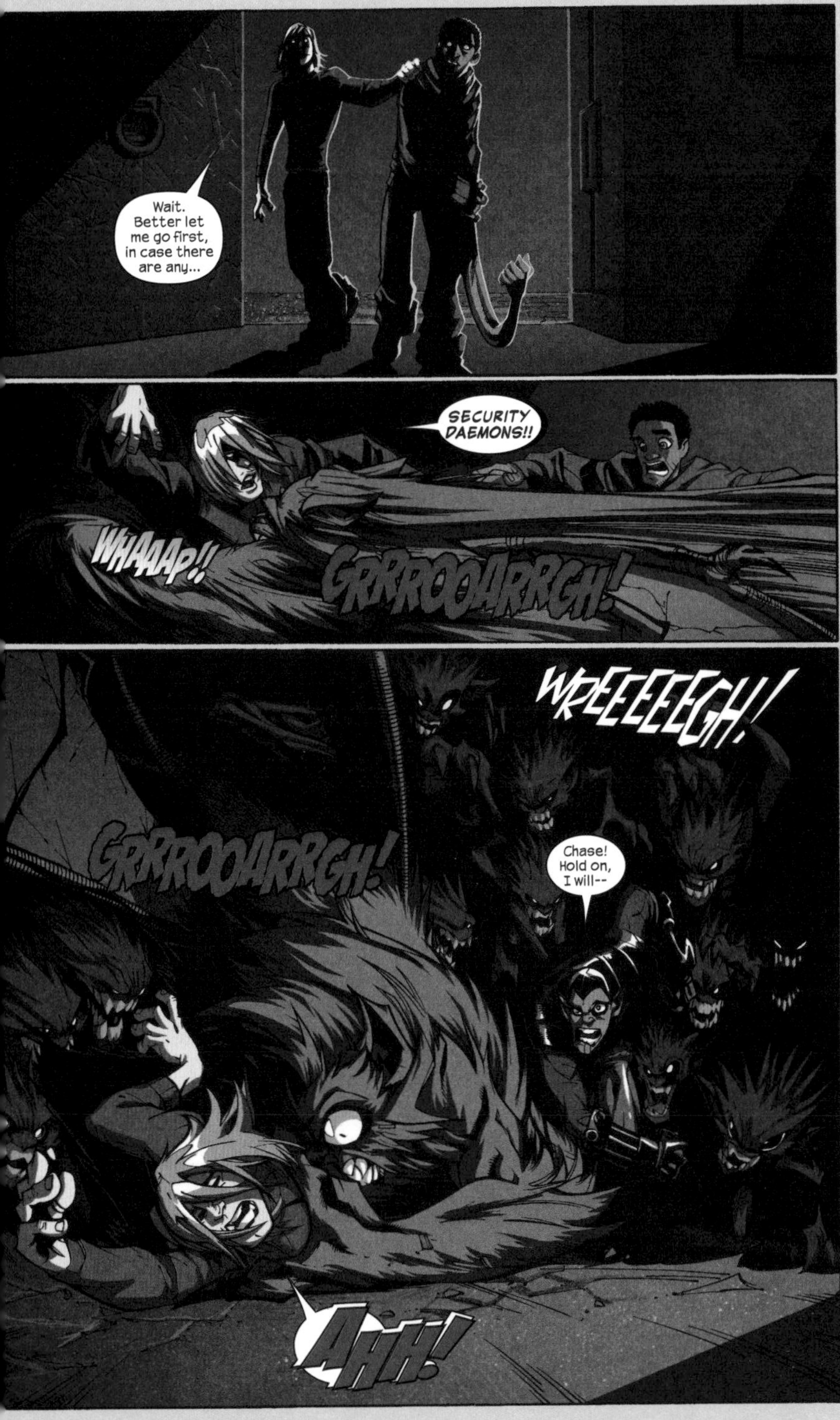

Wait. Better let me go first, in case there are any...
SECURITY DAEMONS!!
WHAAAP!!
GRRROOARRRGH!
WREEEEEEGH!
GRRROOARRRGH!
Chase! Hold on, I will--
AHH!

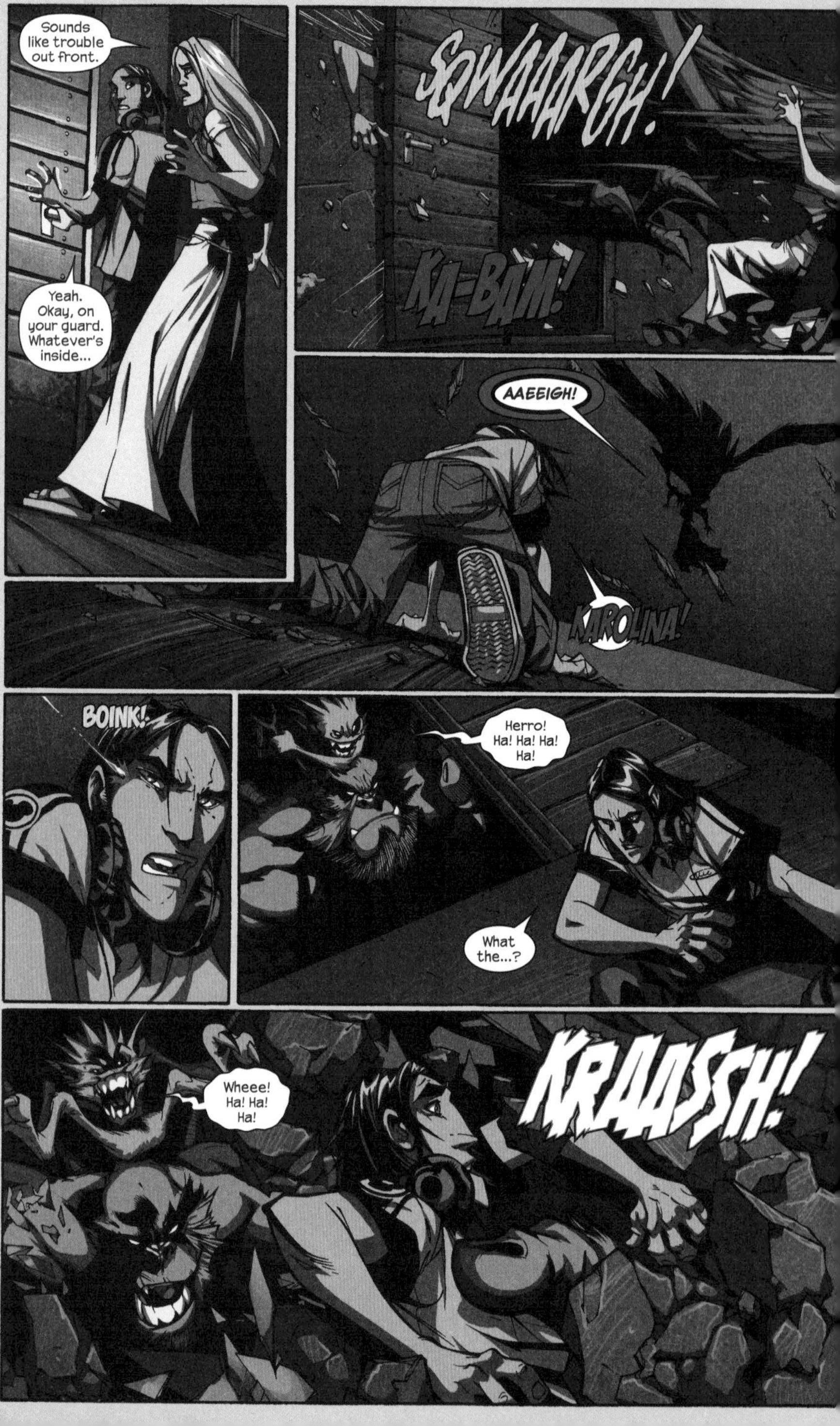

Sounds like trouble out front.
Yeah. Okay, on your guard. Whatever's inside...
SQWAAARGH!
KA-BAM!
AAEEIGH!
KAROLINA!
BOINK!
Herro! Ha! Ha! Ha! Ha!
What the...?
Wheee! Ha! Ha! Ha!
KRAASH!

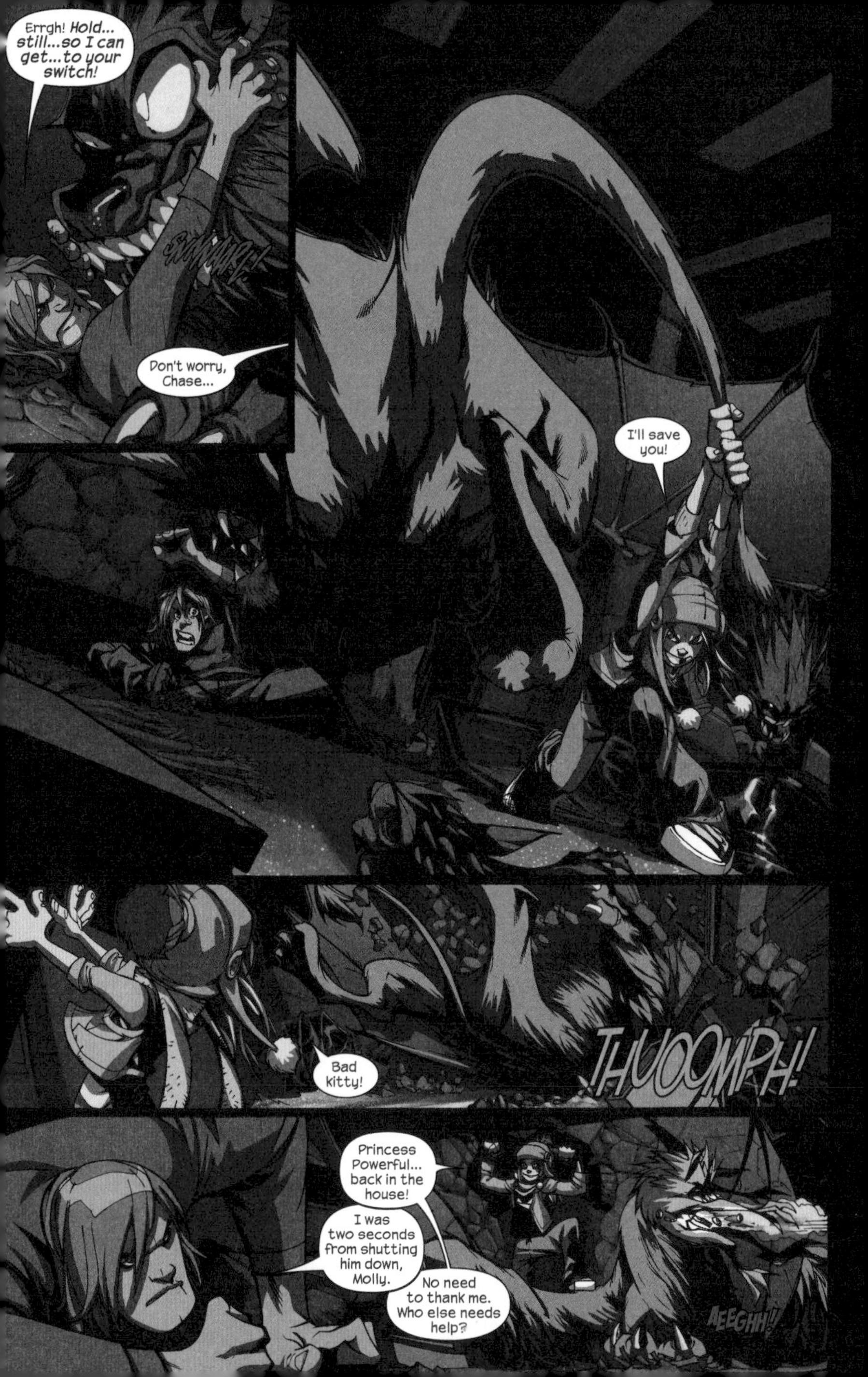
Errgh! Hold... still...so I can get...to your switch!
SKWAARL!
Don't worry, Chase...
I'll save you!
Bad kitty!
THUOOMPH!
Princess Powerful... back in the house!
I was two seconds from shutting him down, Molly.
No need to thank me. Who else needs help?
AEEGHH!!

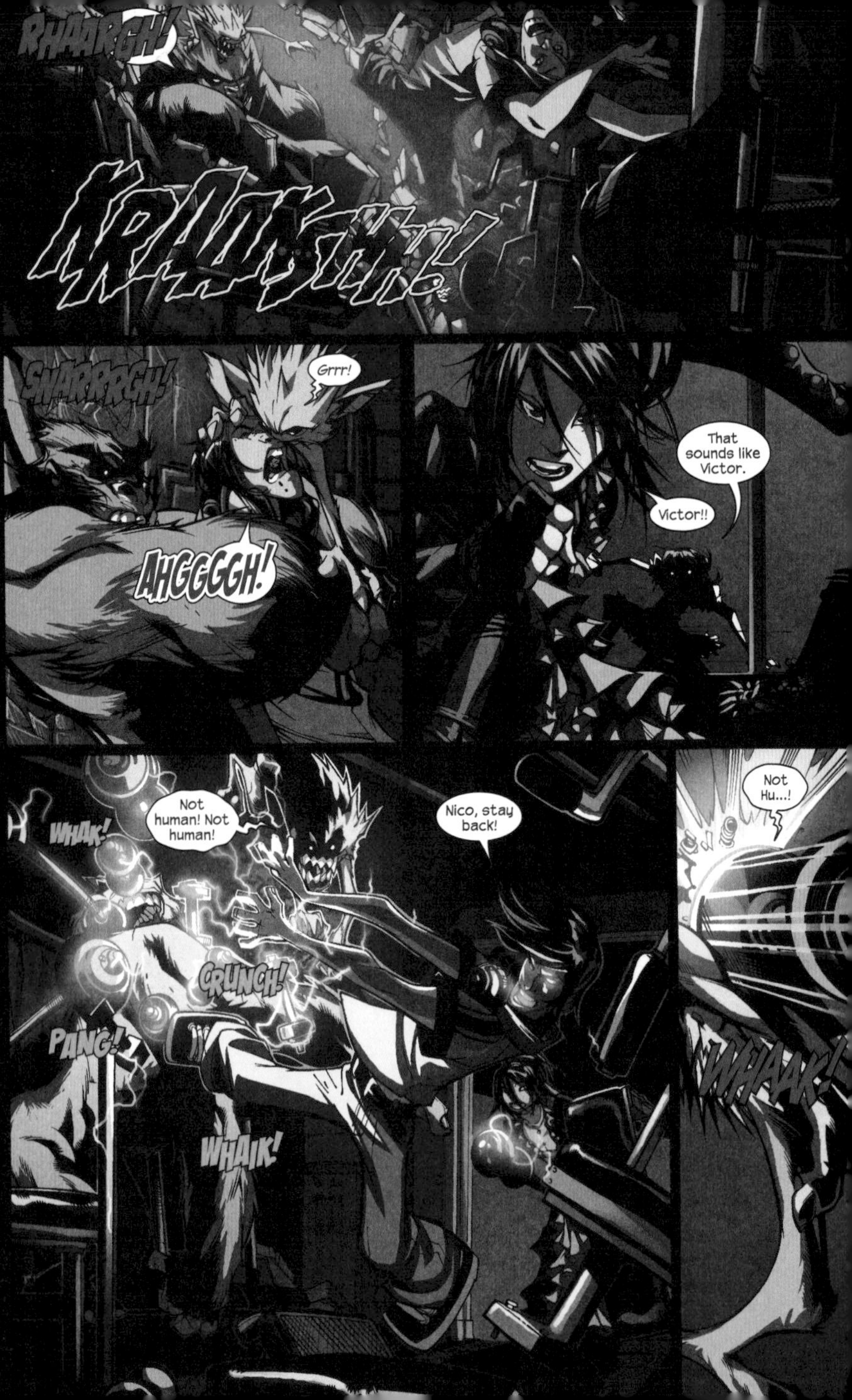
RHAARGH!
KRAASHH!
SHARRRGH!
Grrr!
AHGGGGH!
That sounds like Victor.
Victor!!
WHAK!
Not human! Not human!
Nico, stay back!
CRUNCH!
PANG!
WHAIK!
Not Hu...!
WHAAK!

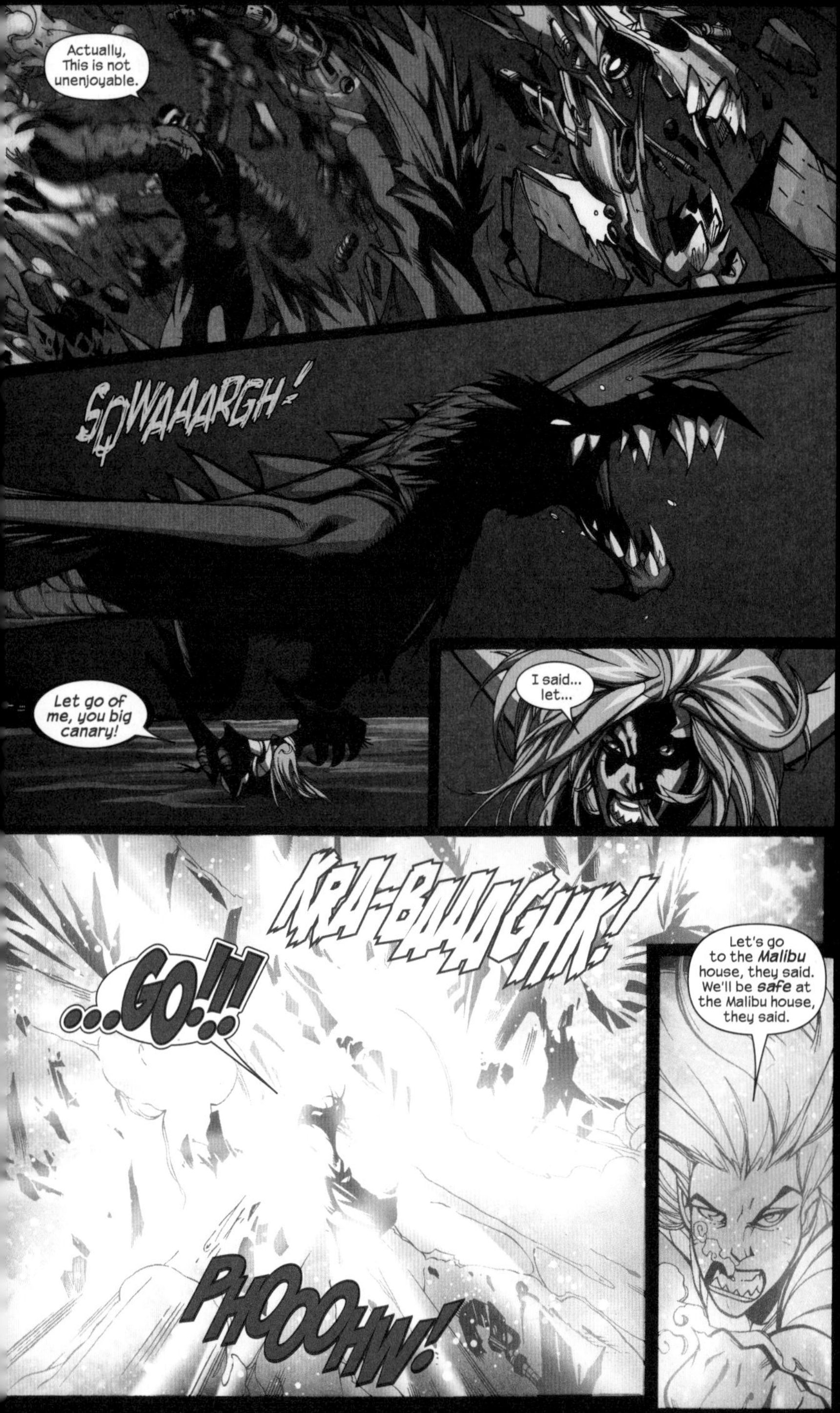

Actually, This is not unenjoyable.
SQWAAARGH!
Let go of me, you big canary!
I said... let...
KRA-BAAAGHK!
...GO!!!
Let's go to the *Malibu* house, they said. We'll be *safe* at the Malibu house, they said.
PHOOOHW!

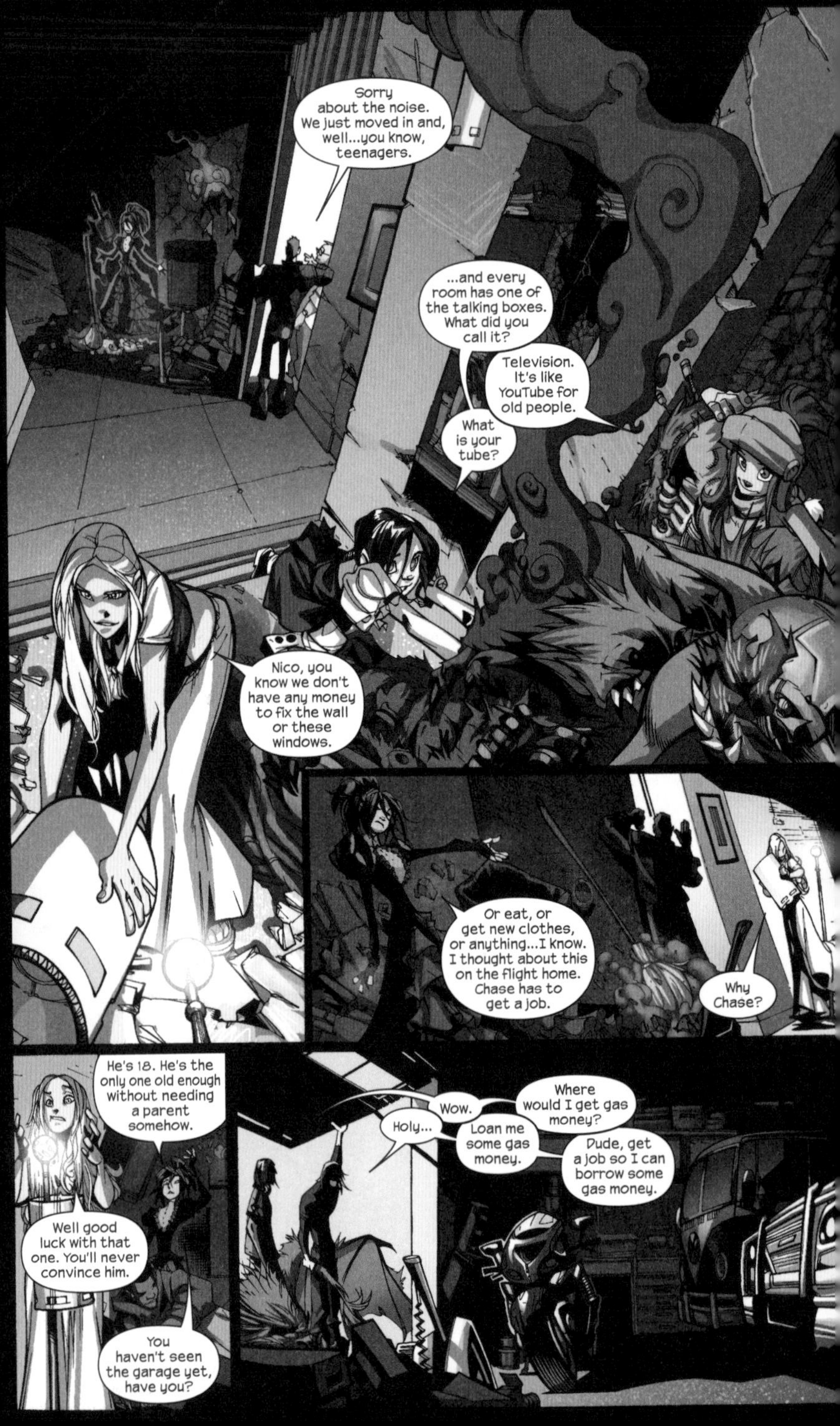
Sorry about the noise. We just moved in and, well...you know, teenagers.
...and every room has one of the talking boxes. What did you call it?
Television. It's like YouTube for old people.
What is your tube?
Nico, you know we don't have any money to fix the wall or these windows.
Or eat, or get new clothes, or anything...I know. I thought about this on the flight home. Chase has to get a job.
Why Chase?
He's 18. He's the only one old enough without needing a parent somehow.
Well good luck with that one. You'll never convince him.
You haven't seen the garage yet, have you?
Wow.
Holy...
Where would I get gas money?
Loan me some gas money.
Dude, get a job so I can borrow some gas money.

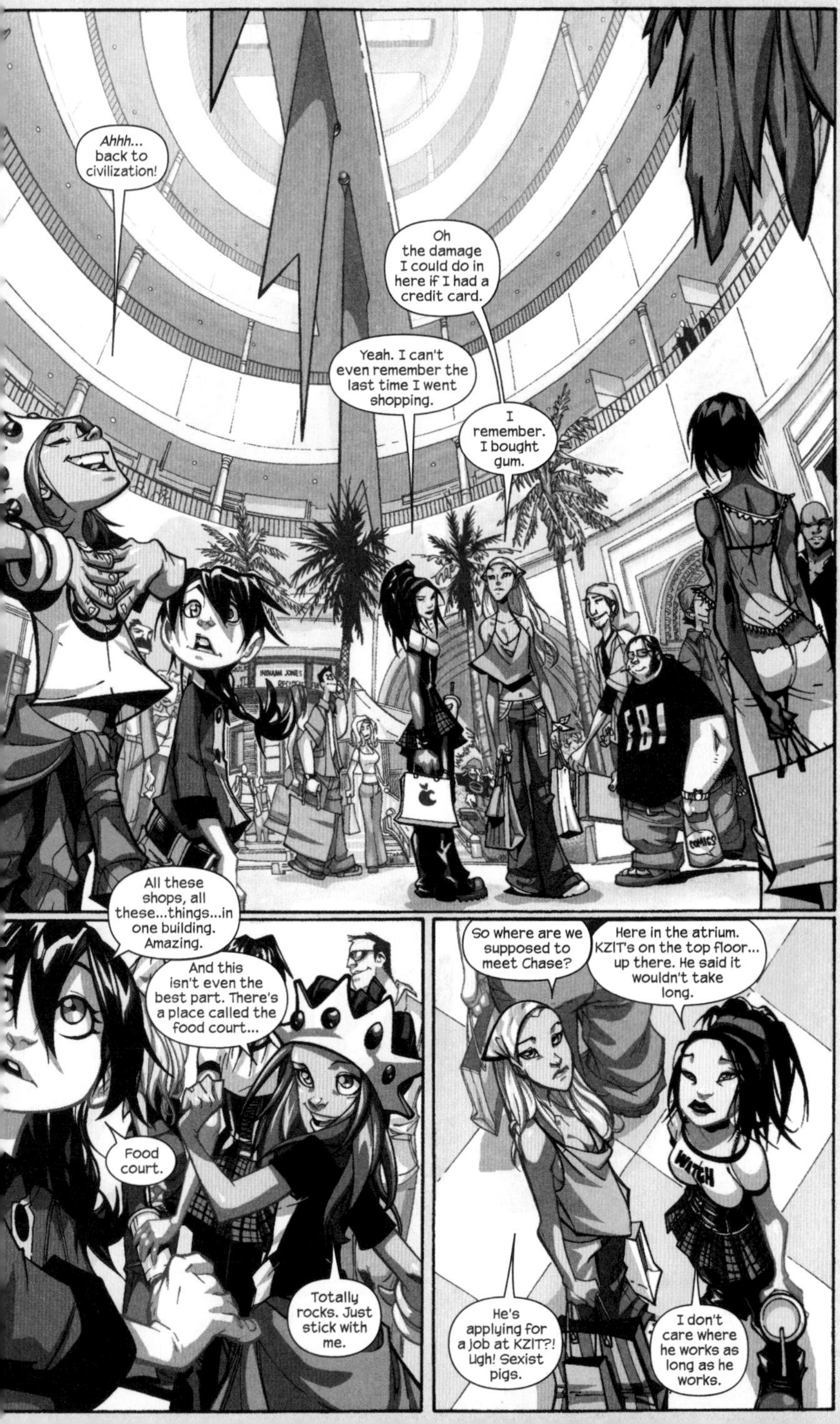

Ahhh... back to civilization!
Oh the damage I could do in here if I had a credit card.
Yeah. I can't even remember the last time I went shopping.
I remember. I bought gum.
COMICS
All these shops, all these...things...in one building. Amazing.
And this isn't even the best part. There's a place called the food court...
Food court.
Totally rocks. Just stick with me.
So where are we supposed to meet Chase?
Here in the atrium. KZIT's on the top floor... up there. He said it wouldn't take long.
WATCH
He's applying for a job at KZIT?! Ugh! Sexist pigs.
I don't care where he works as long as he works.

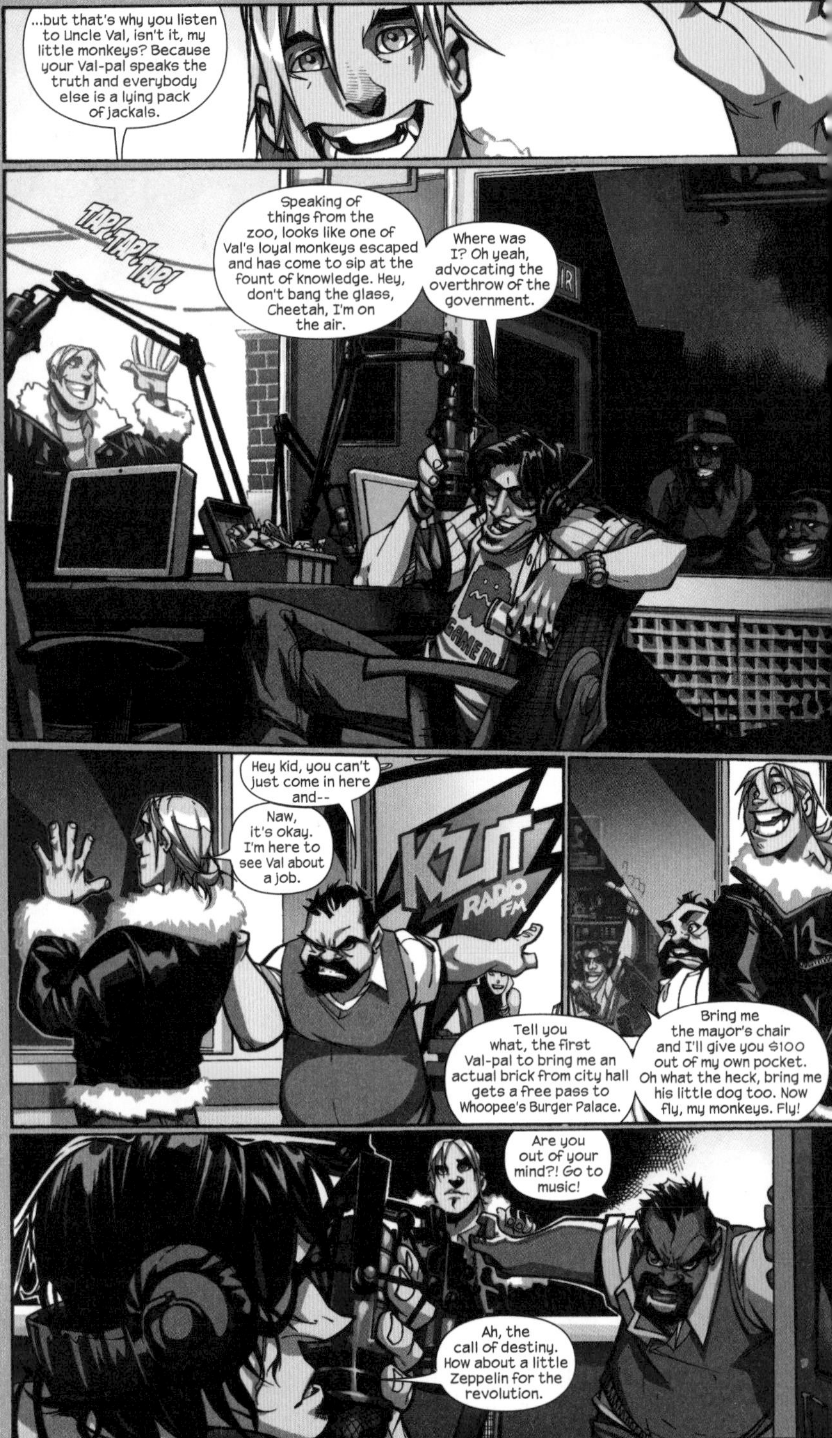

...but that's why you listen to Uncle Val, isn't it, my little monkeys? Because your Val-pal speaks the truth and everybody else is a lying pack of jackals.
TAP! TAP! TAP!
Speaking of things from the zoo, looks like one of Val's loyal monkeys escaped and has come to sip at the fount of knowledge. Hey, don't bang the glass, Cheetah, I'm on the air.
Where was I? Oh yeah, advocating the overthrow of the government.
Hey kid, you can't just come in here and--
Naw, it's okay. I'm here to see Val about a job.
KZTT RADIO FM
Tell you what, the first Val-pal to bring me an actual brick from city hall gets a free pass to Whoopee's Burger Palace.
Bring me the mayor's chair and I'll give you $100 out of my own pocket. Oh what the heck, bring me his little dog too. Now fly, my monkeys. Fly!
Are you out of your mind?! Go to music!
Ah, the call of destiny. How about a little Zeppelin for the revolution.

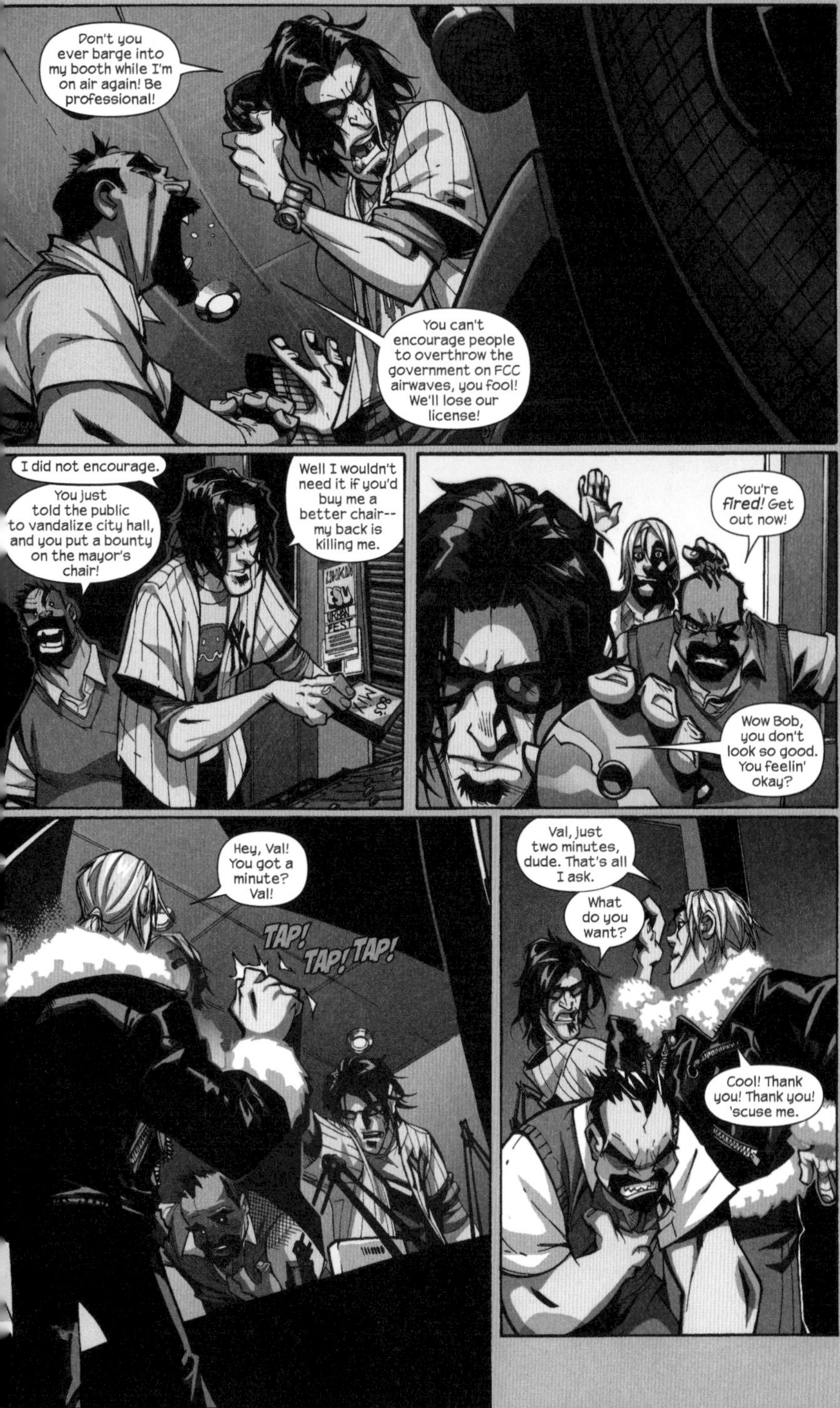

Don't you ever barge into my booth while I'm on air again! Be professional!
You can't encourage people to overthrow the government on FCC airwaves, you fool! We'll lose our license!
I did not encourage.
You just told the public to vandalize city hall, and you put a bounty on the mayor's chair!
Well I wouldn't need it if you'd buy me a better chair-- my back is killing me.
80's MIX
You're *fired!* Get out now!
Wow Bob, you don't look so good. You feelin' okay?
Hey, Val! You got a minute? Val!
TAP! TAP! TAP!
Val, just two minutes, dude. That's all I ask.
What do you want?
Cool! Thank you! Thank you! 'scuse me.

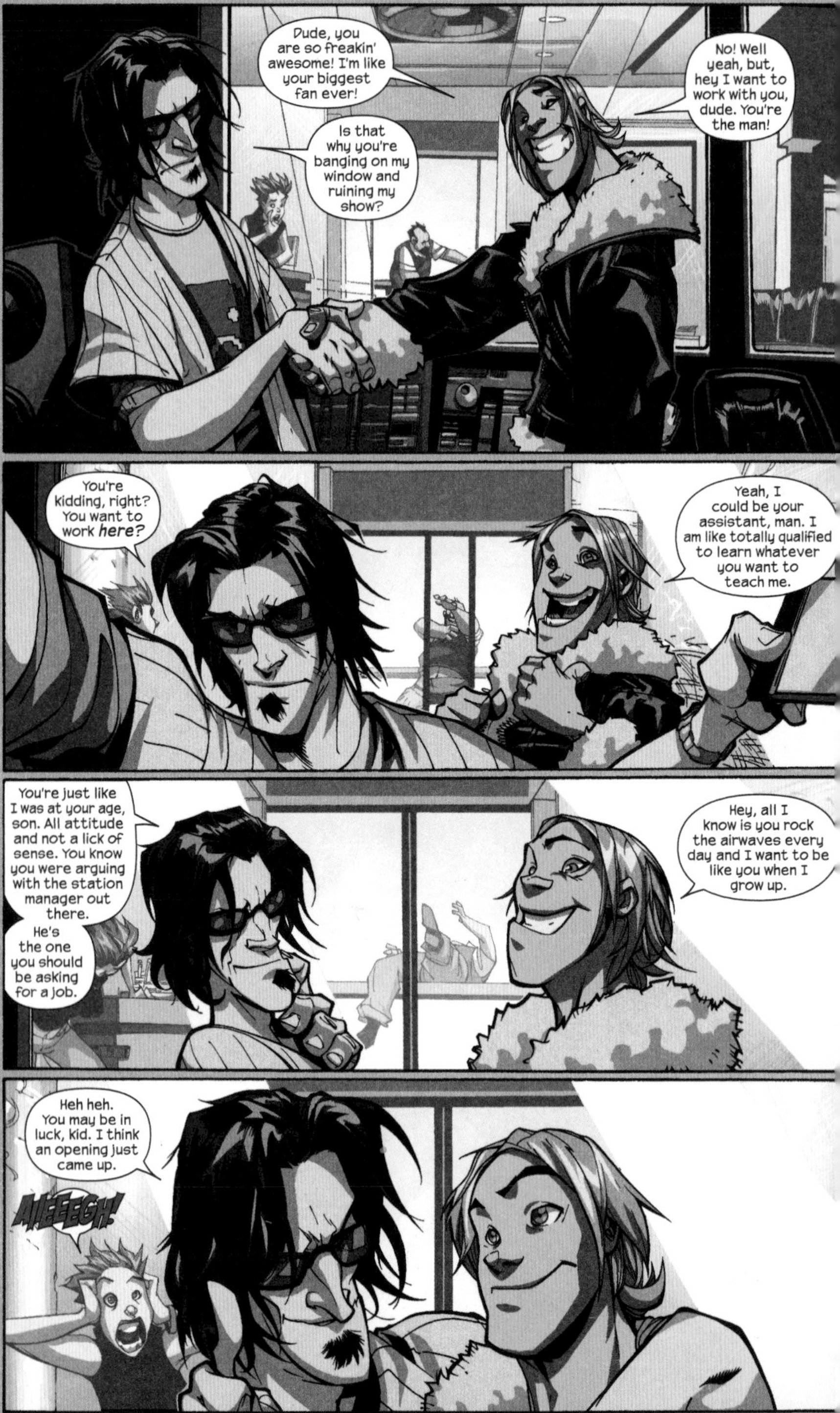
Dude, you are so freakin' awesome! I'm like your biggest fan ever!
Is that why you're banging on my window and ruining my show?
No! Well yeah, but, hey I want to work with you, dude. You're the man!
You're kidding, right? You want to work *here?*
Yeah, I could be your assistant, man. I am like totally qualified to learn whatever you want to teach me.
You're just like I was at your age, son. All attitude and not a lick of sense. You know you were arguing with the station manager out there.
He's the one you should be asking for a job.
Hey, all I know is you rock the airwaves every day and I want to be like you when I grow up.
Heh heh. You may be in luck, kid. I think an opening just came up.
AIIEEEGH!

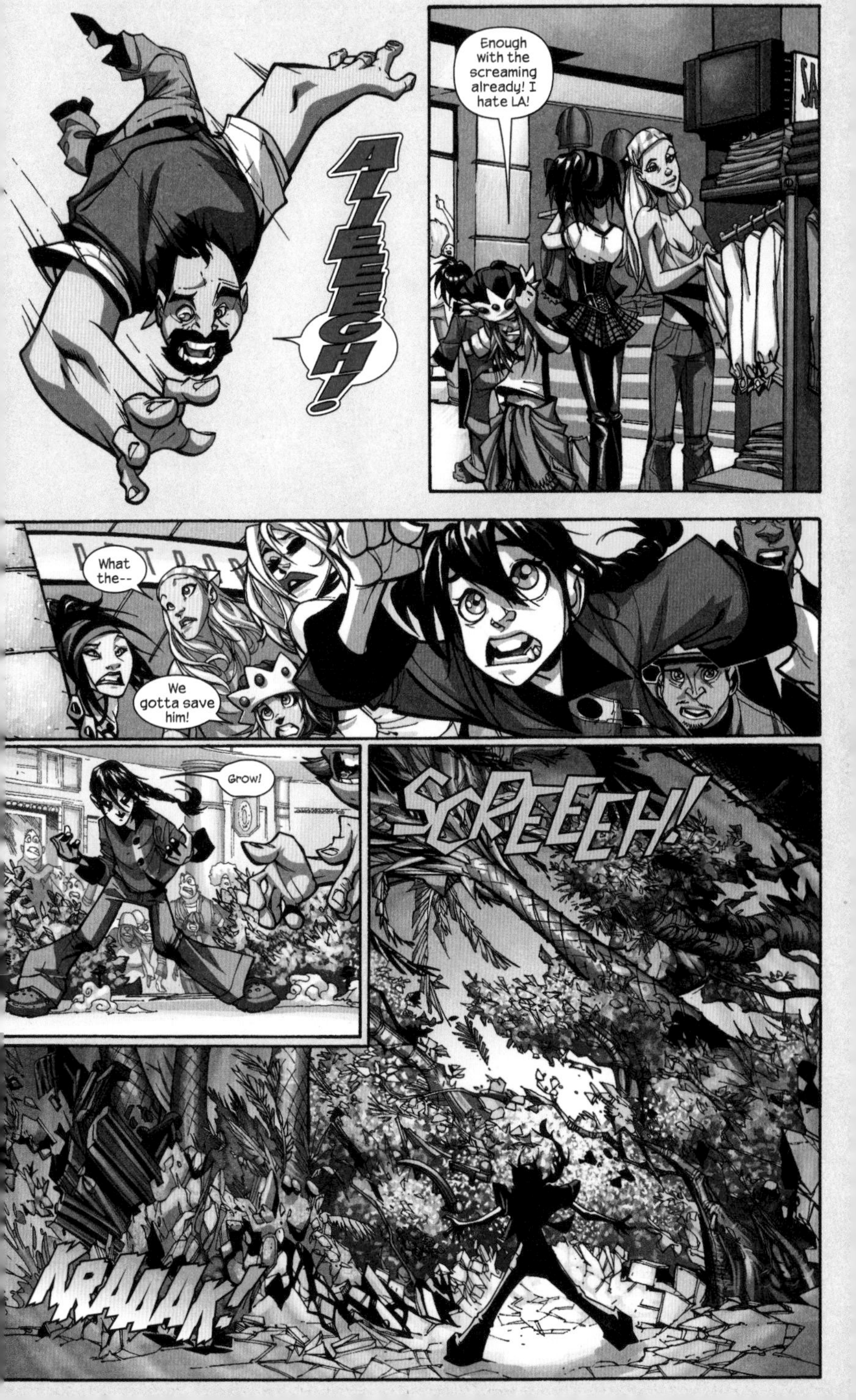
AIIEEEGH!
Enough with the screaming already! I hate LA!
What the--
We gotta save him!
Grow!
SCREEEEH!
KRAAAK!

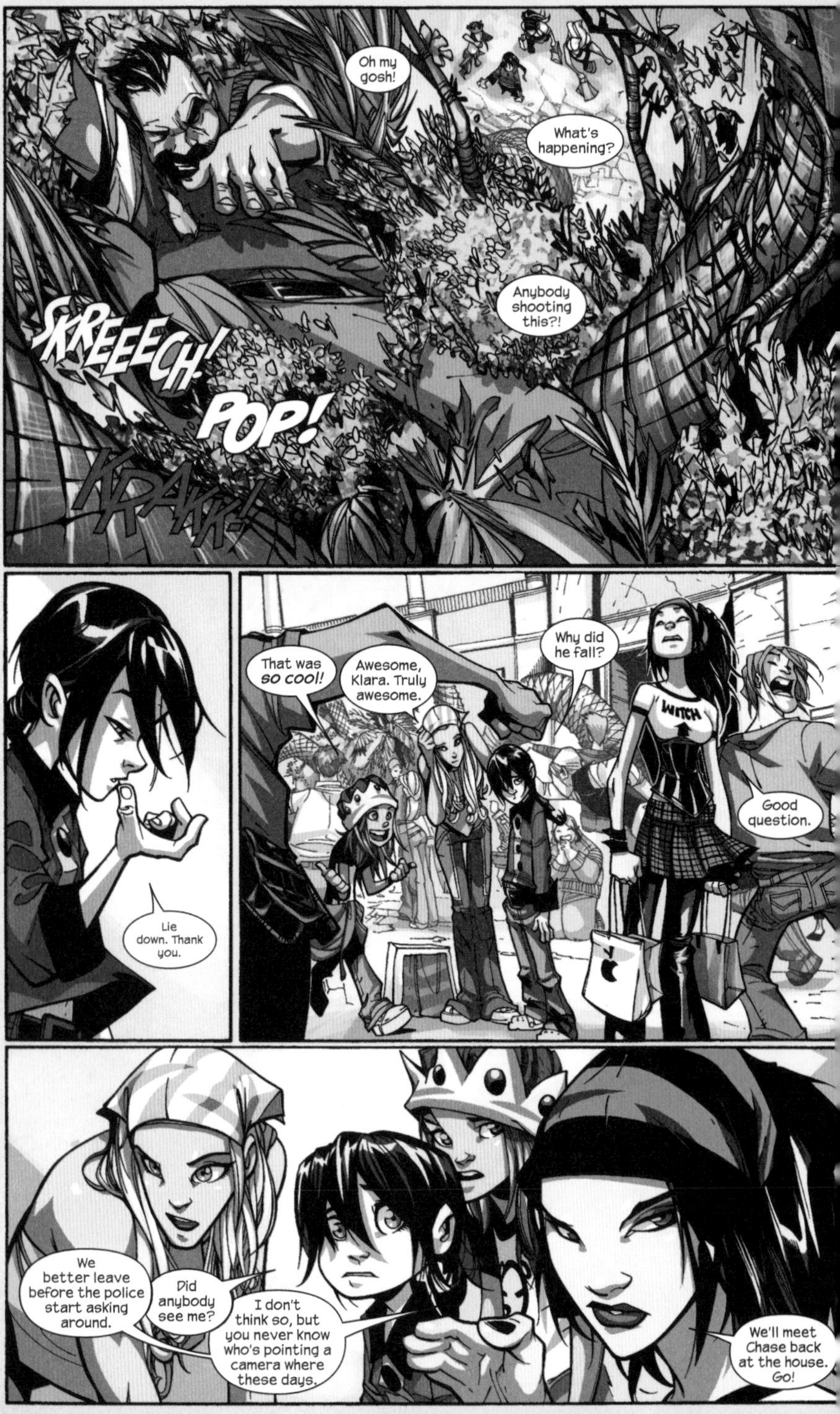

Oh my gosh!
What's happening?
Anybody shooting this?!
SKREEECH!
POP!
KRAKK!
Lie down. Thank you.
That was *so cool!*
Awesome, Klara. Truly awesome.
Why did he fall?
Good question.
We better leave before the police start asking around.
Did anybody see me?
I don't think so, but you never know who's pointing a camera where these days.
We'll meet Chase back at the house. Go!

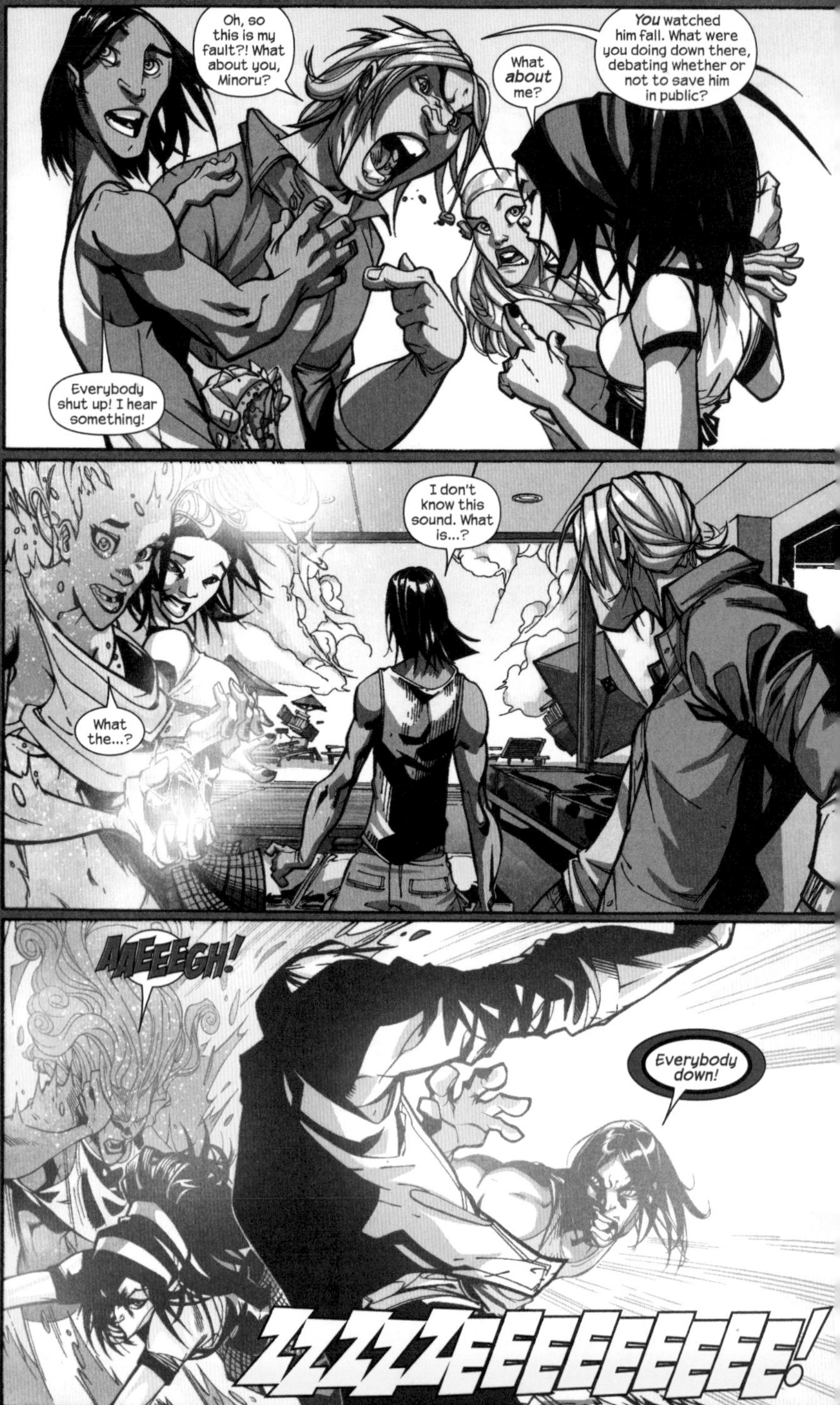
Oh, so this is my fault?! What about you, Minoru?
What about me?
You watched him fall. What were you doing down there, debating whether or not to save him in public?
Everybody shut up! I hear something!
I don't know this sound. What is...?
What the...?
AAEEEGH!
Everybody down!
ZZZZZEEEEEEEEEE!

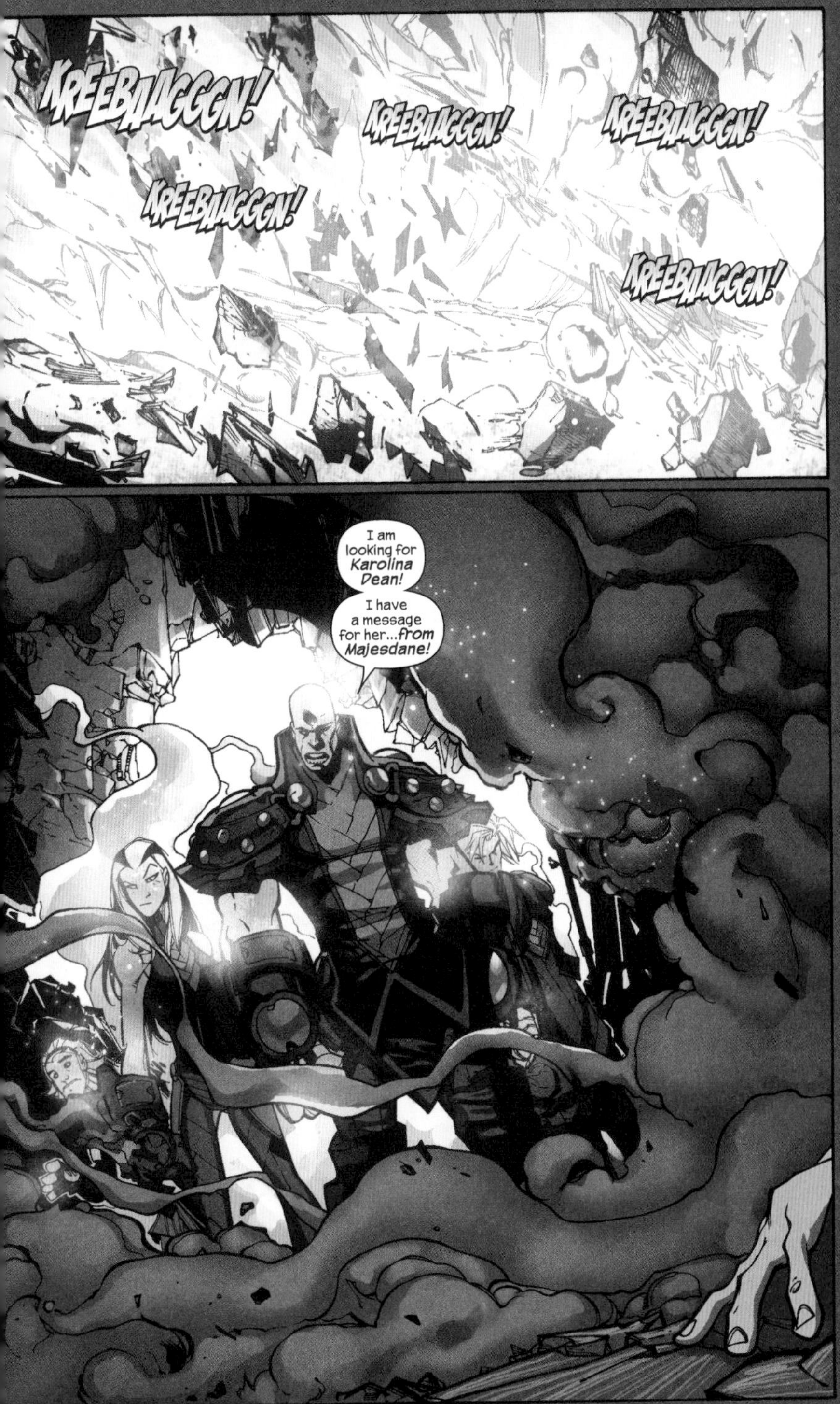
KREEBAAGGGN!
KREEBAAGGGN!
KREEBAAGGGN!
KREEBAAGGGN!
KREEBAAGGGN!
I am looking for Karolina Dean!
I have a message for her...from Majesdane!

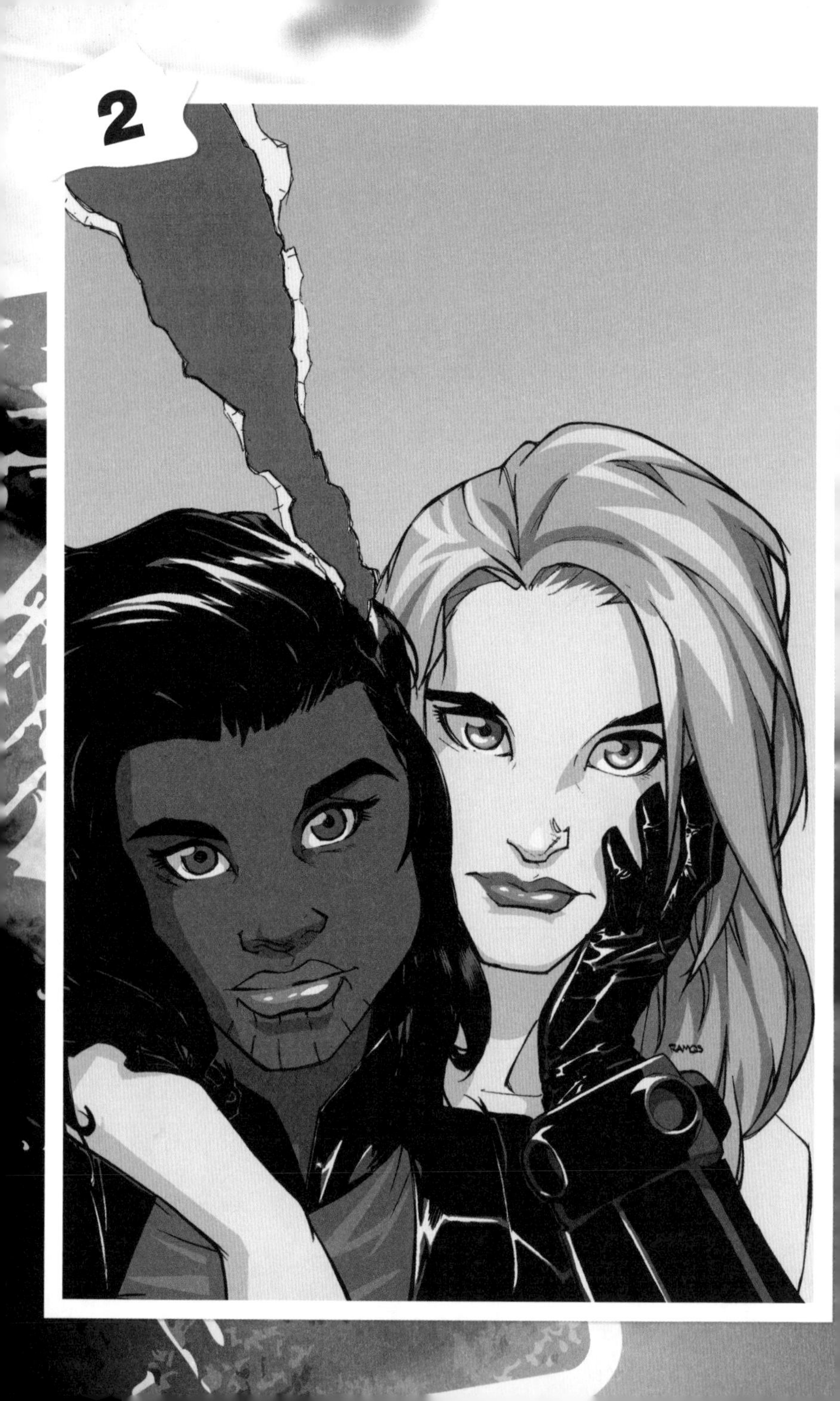
2
RAMOS

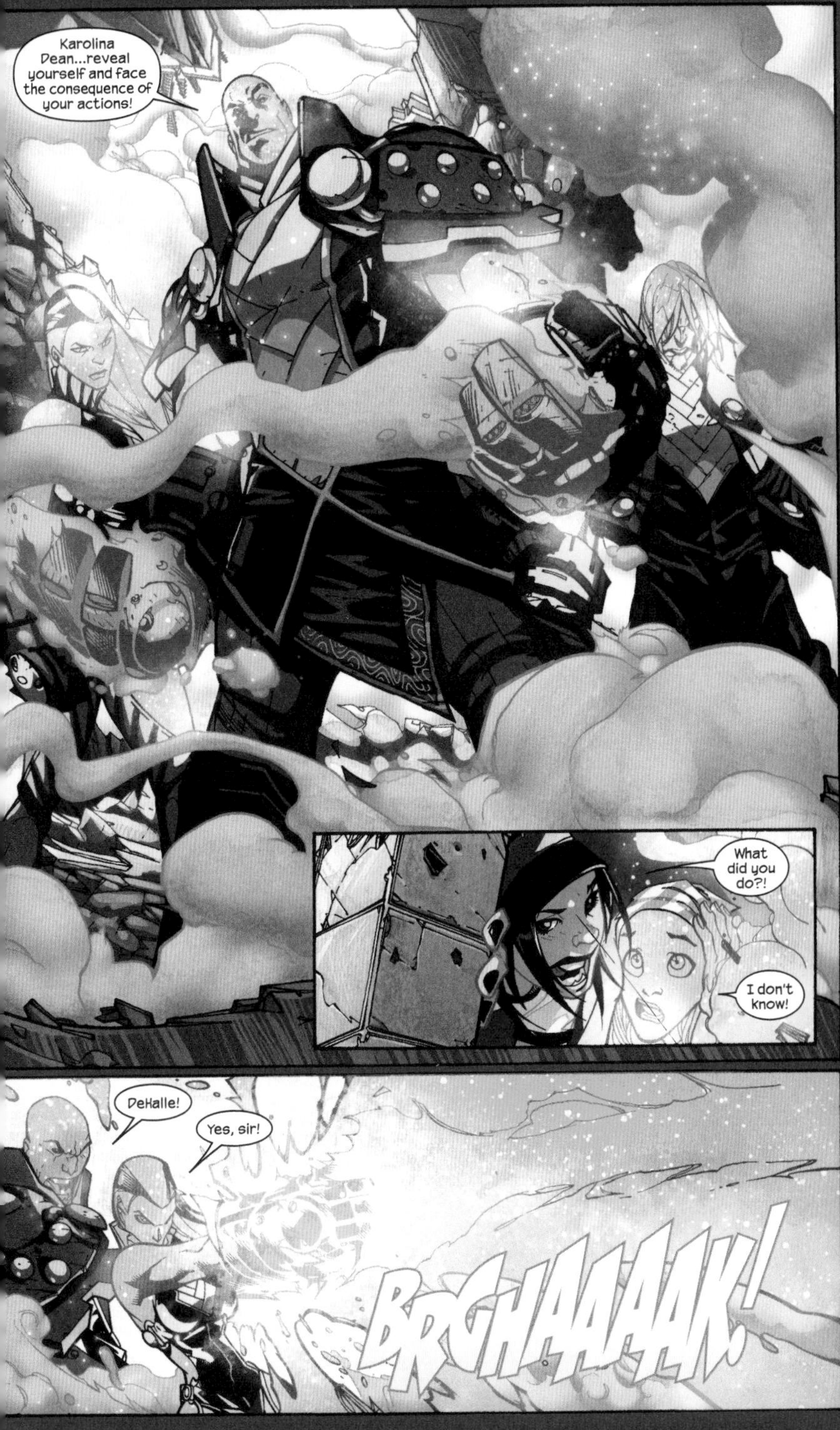
Karolina Dean...reveal yourself and face the consequence of your actions!
What did you do?!
I don't know!
DeHalle!
Yes, sir!
BRCHAAAAK!

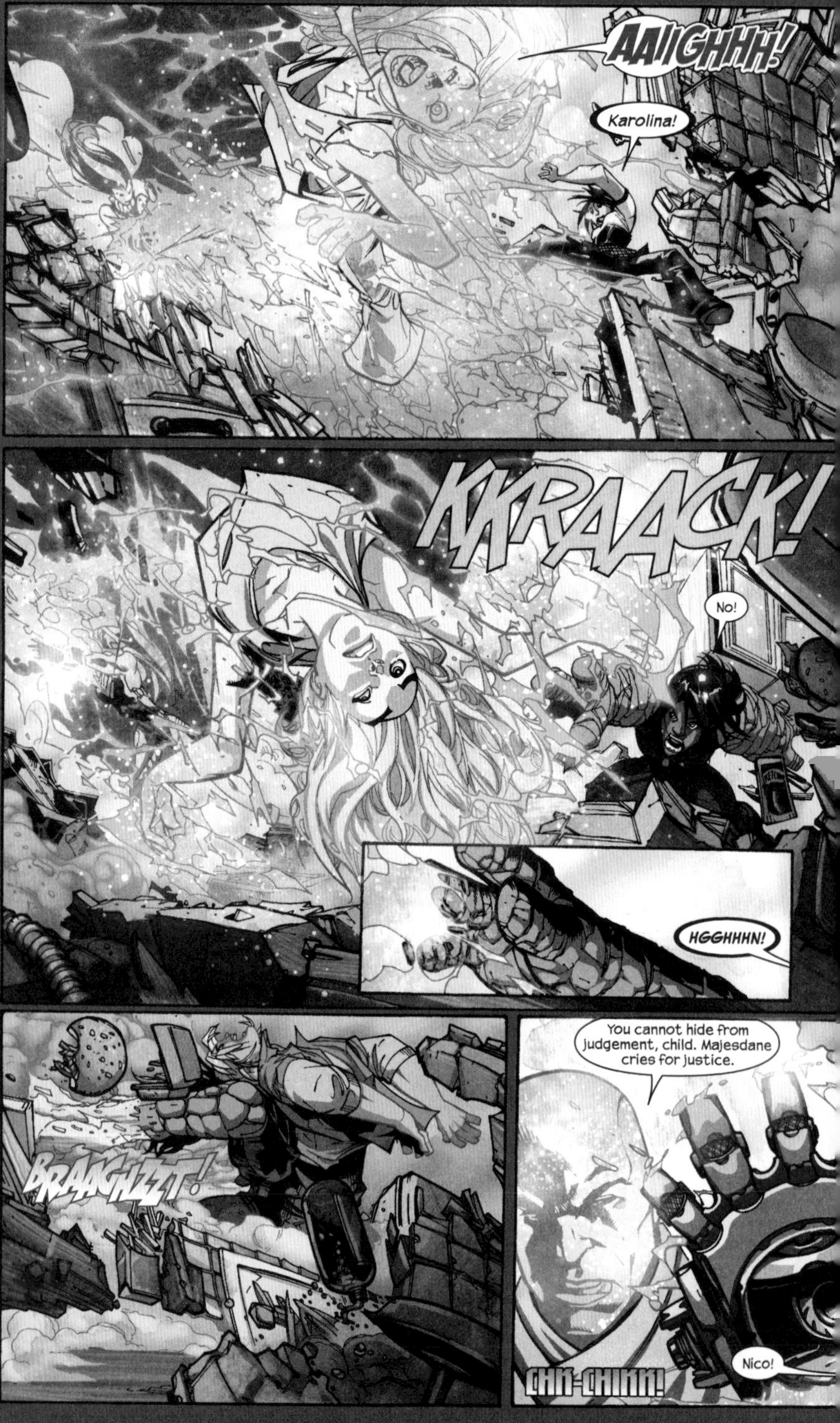
AAIIGHHH!
Karolina!
KKRAACK!
No!
HGGHHHN!
BRAAGHZZT!
You cannot hide from judgement, child. Majesdane cries for justice.
CHK-CHIKK!
Nico!

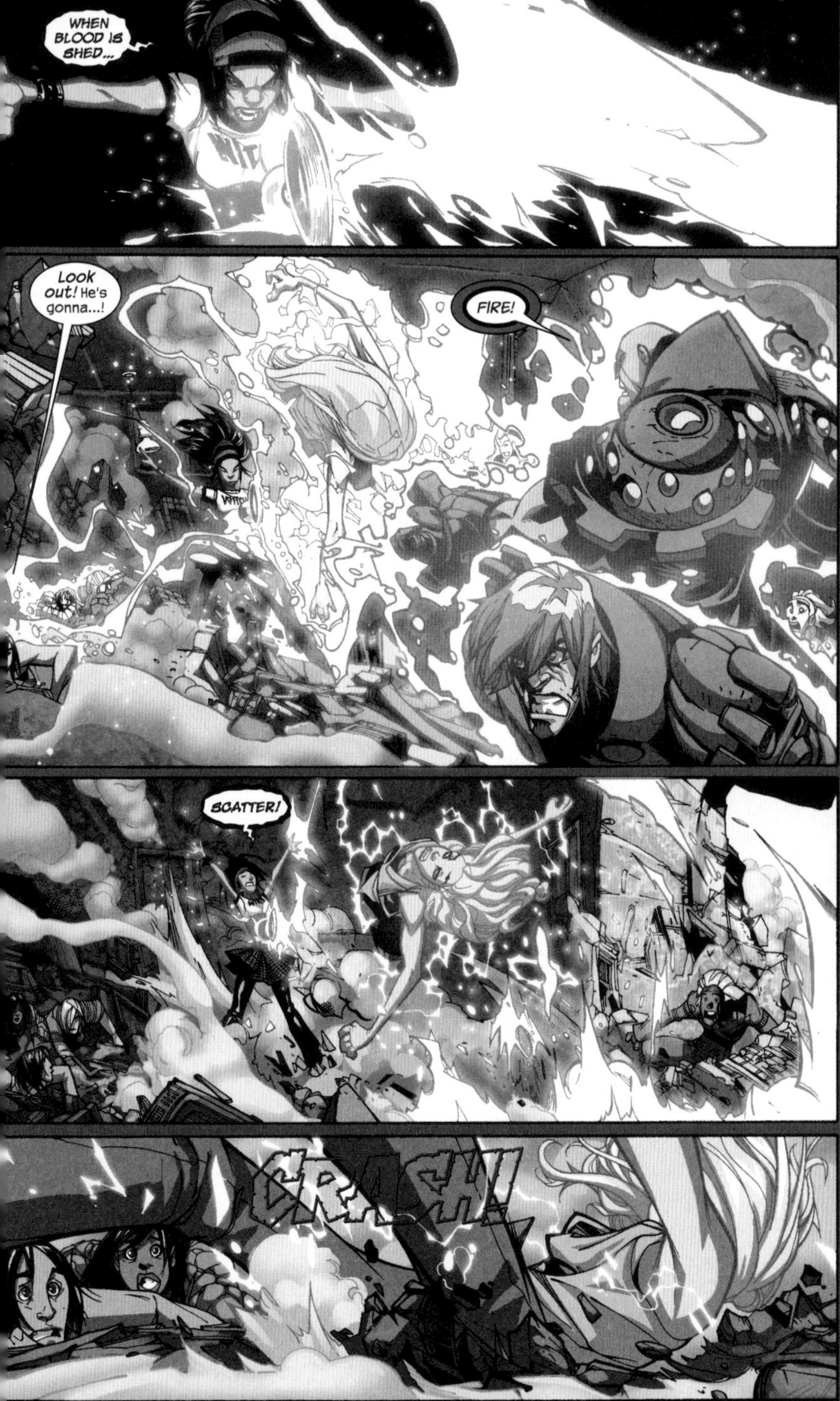

WHEN BLOOD IS SHED...
Look out! He's gonna...!
FIRE!
SCATTER!
CRASH!

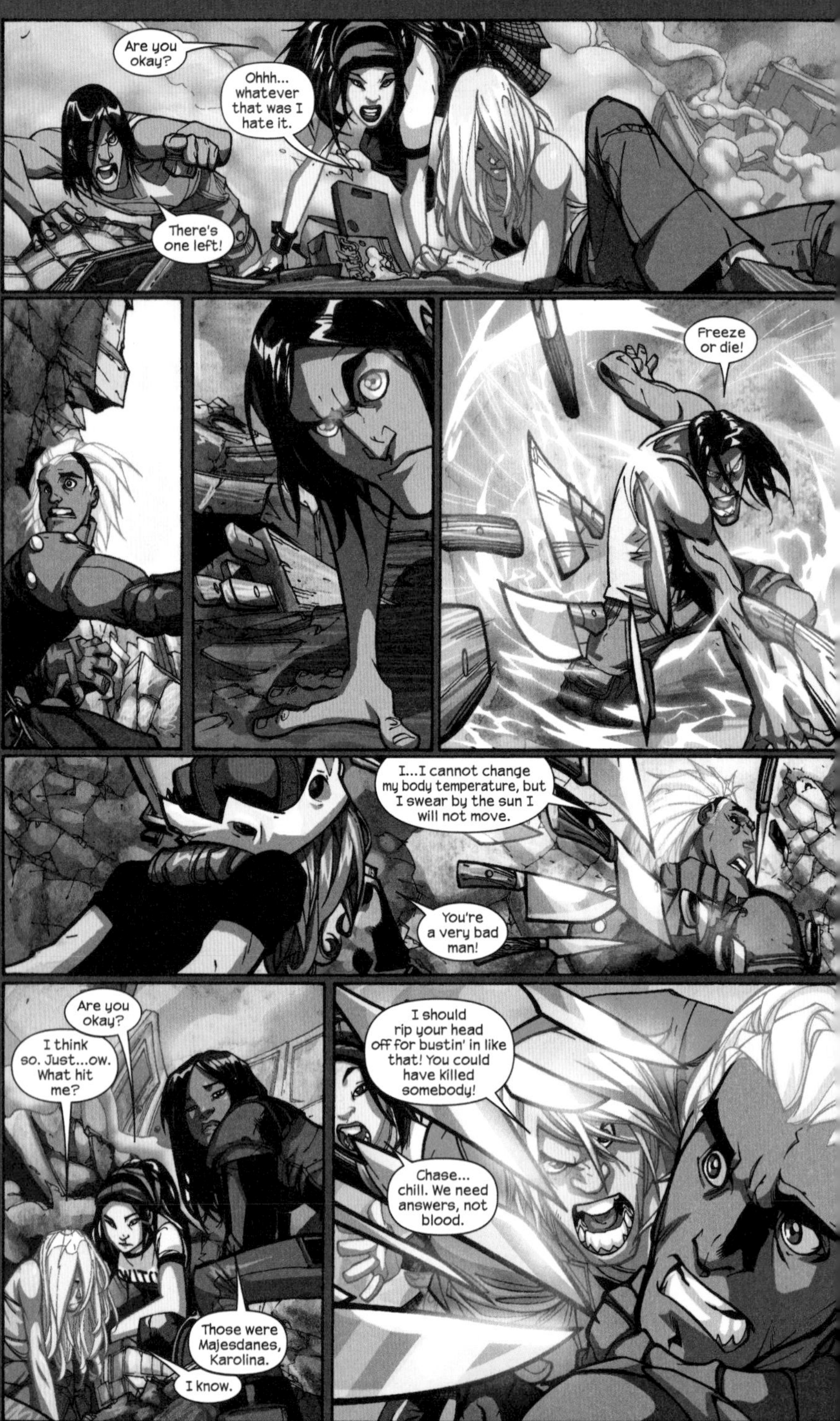
Are you okay?
Ohhh... whatever that was I hate it.
There's one left!
Freeze or die!
I...I cannot change my body temperature, but I swear by the sun I will not move.
You're a very bad man!
Are you okay?
I think so. Just...ow. What hit me?
Those were Majesdanes, Karolina.
I know.
I should rip your head off for bustin' in like that! You could have killed somebody!
Chase... chill. We need answers, not blood.

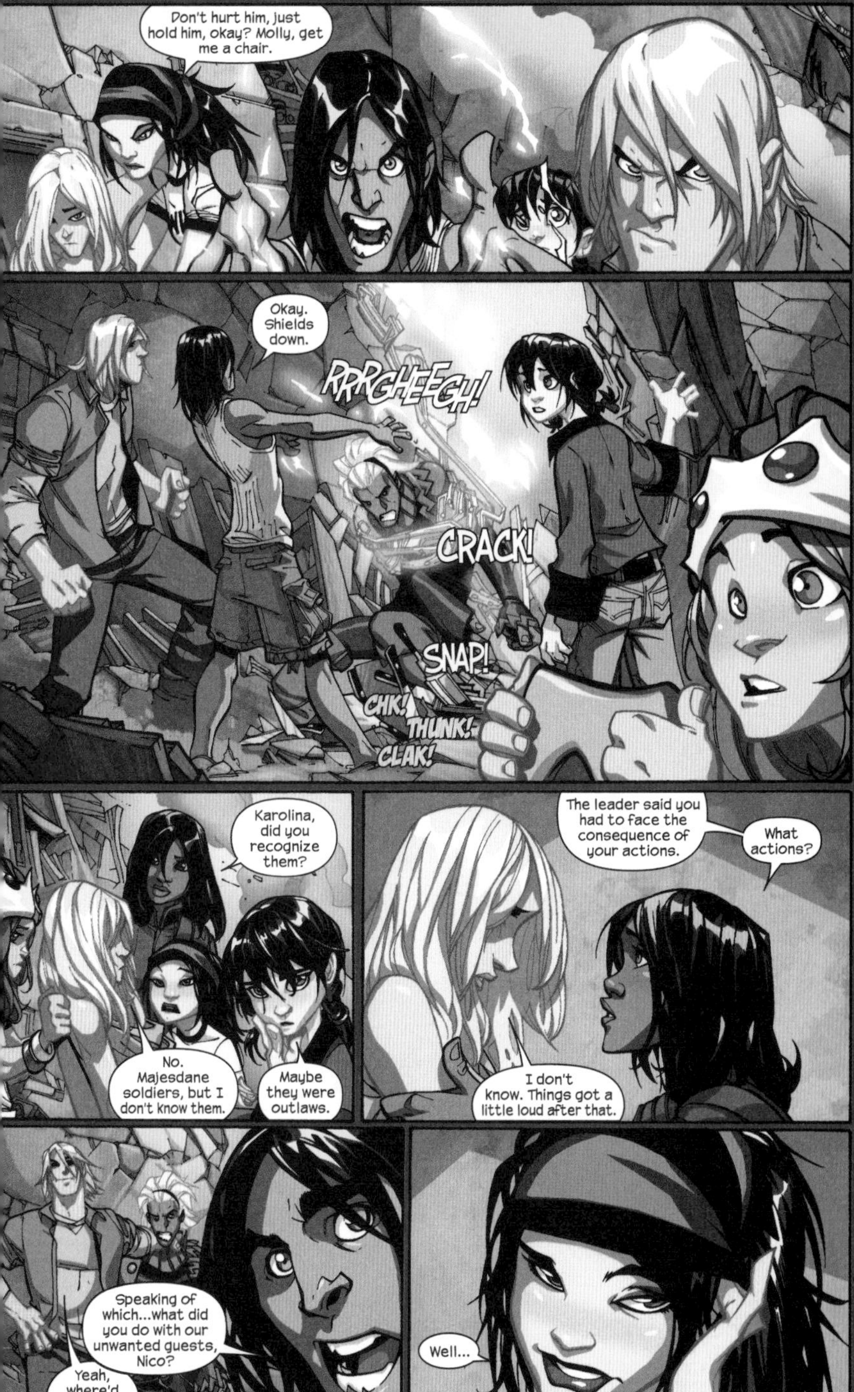

Don't hurt him, just hold him, okay? Molly, get me a chair.
Okay. Shields down.
RRRGHEEGH!
CRACK!
SNAP!
CHK!
THUNK!
CLAK!
Karolina, did you recognize them?
No. Majesdane soldiers, but I don't know them.
Maybe they were outlaws.
The leader said you had to face the consequence of your actions.
What actions?
I don't know. Things got a little loud after that.
Speaking of which...what did you do with our unwanted guests, Nico?
Yeah, where'd everybody go?
Well...

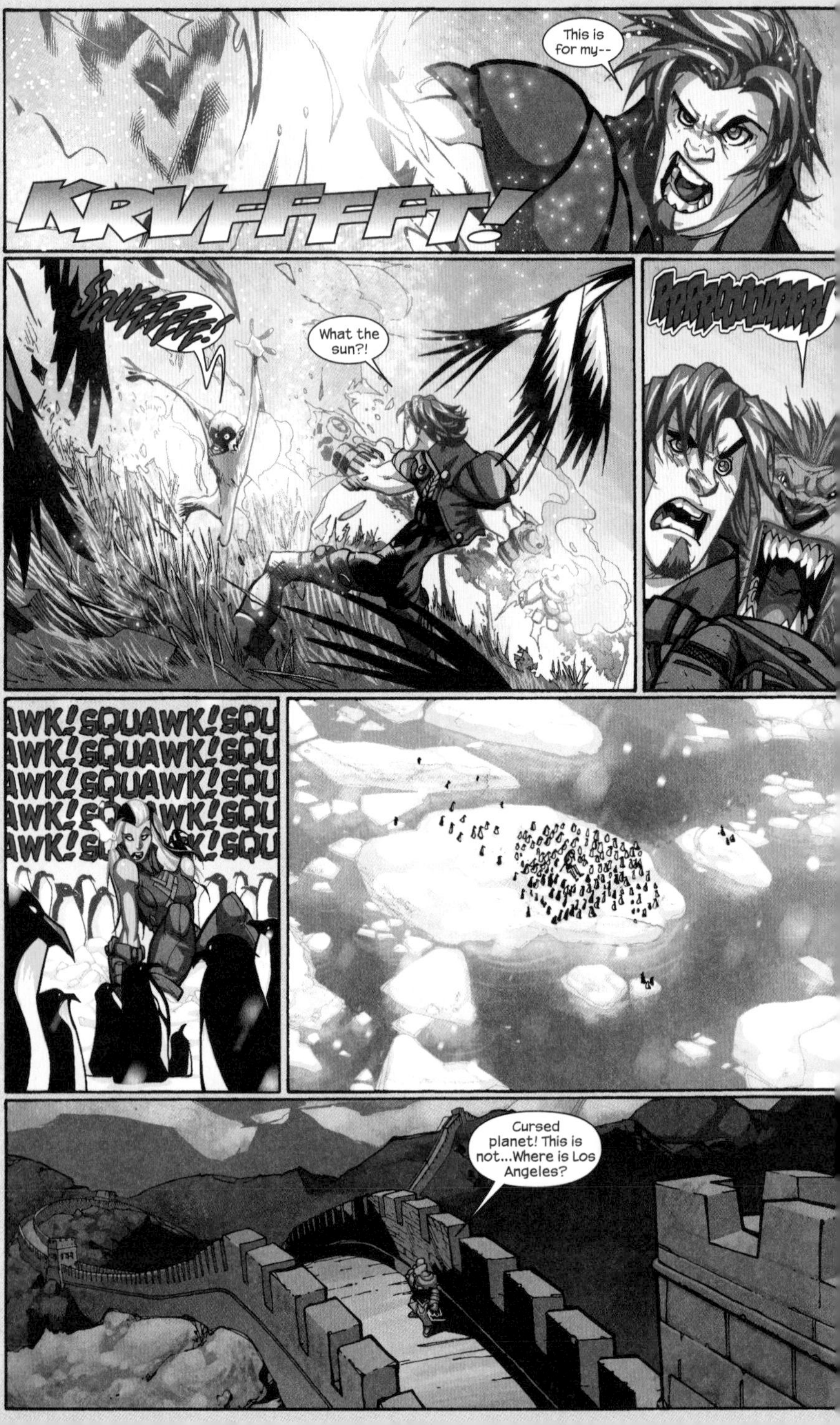
This is for my--
KRVFFFFT!
SQUEEEEEE!
What the sun?!
RRRRROOOUUURRR!
AWK! SQUAWK! SQU
AWK! SQUAWK! SQU
AWK! SQUAWK! SQU
AWK! SQUAWK! SQU
AWK! SQUAWK! SQU
Cursed planet! This is not...Where is Los Angeles?

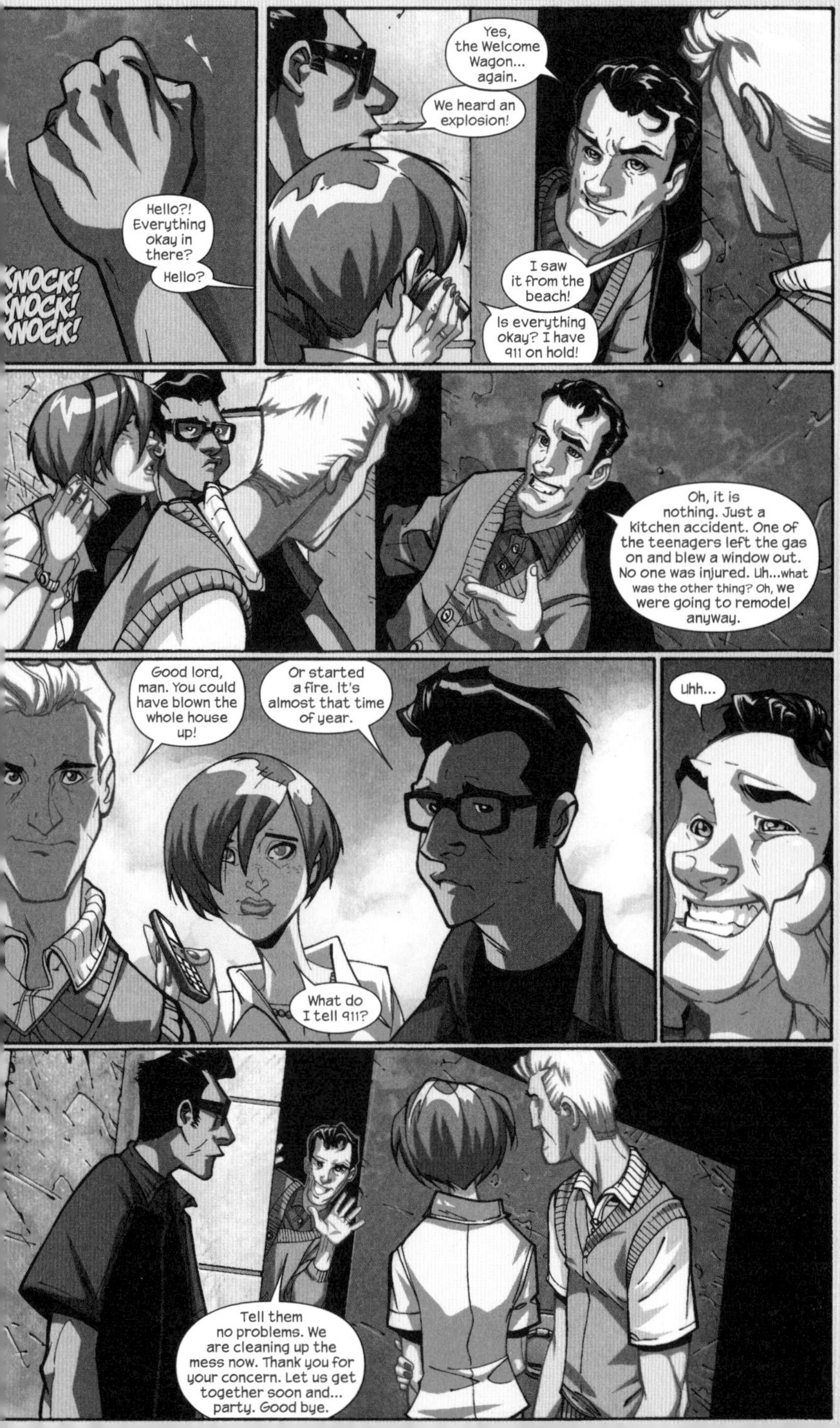

Hello?! Everything okay in there?
Hello?
KNOCK! KNOCK! KNOCK!
Yes, the Welcome Wagon... again.
We heard an explosion!
I saw it from the beach!
Is everything okay? I have 911 on hold!
Oh, it is nothing. Just a kitchen accident. One of the teenagers left the gas on and blew a window out. No one was injured. Uh...what was the other thing? Oh, we were going to remodel anyway.
Good lord, man. You could have blown the whole house up!
Or started a fire. It's almost that time of year.
Uhh...
What do I tell 911?
Tell them no problems. We are cleaning up the mess now. Thank you for your concern. Let us get together soon and... party. Good bye.

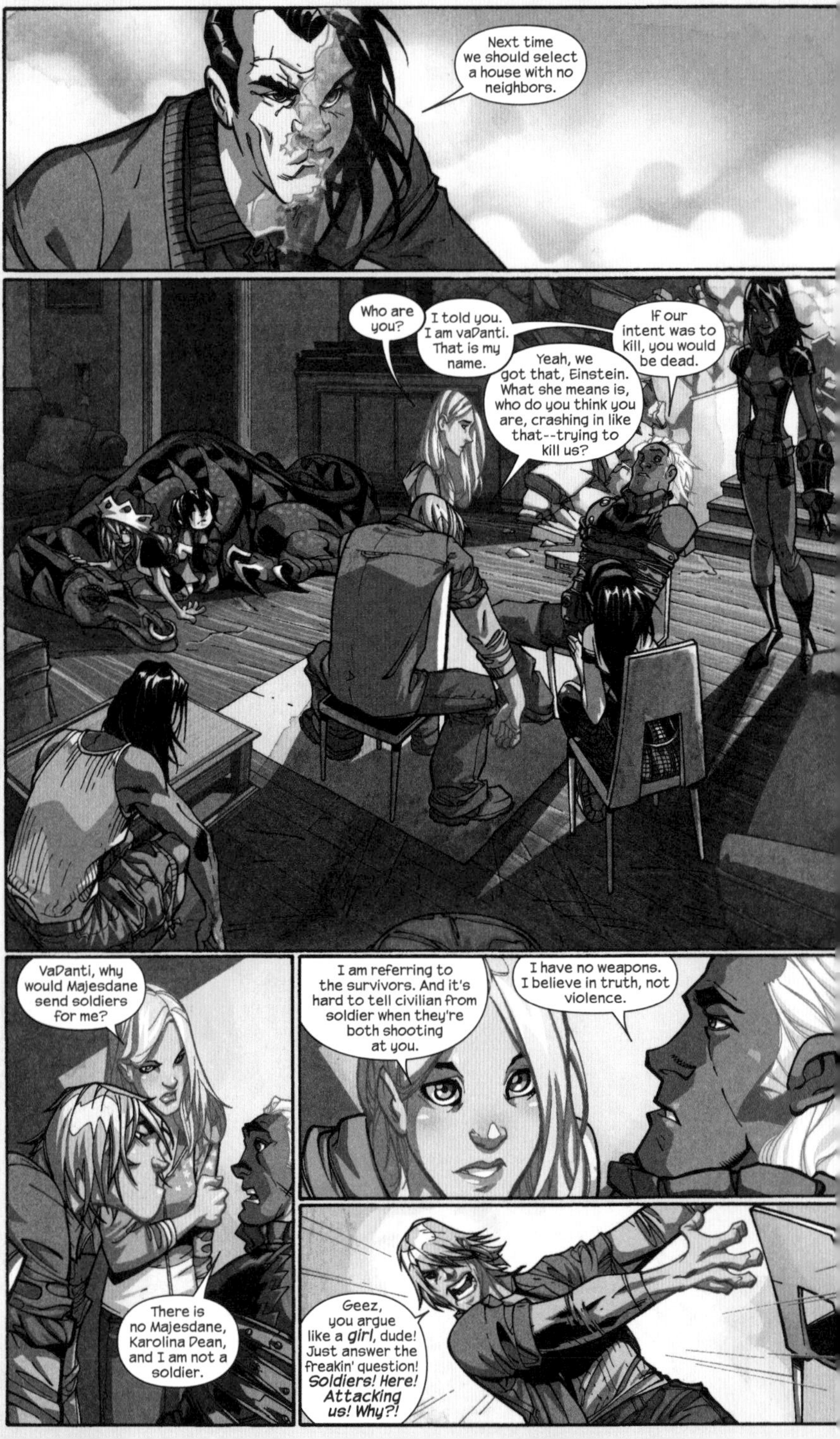

Next time we should select a house with no neighbors.
Who are you?
I told you. I am vaDanti. That is my name.
If our intent was to kill, you would be dead.
Yeah, we got that, Einstein. What she means is, who do you think you are, crashing in like that--trying to kill us?
VaDanti, why would Majesdane send soldiers for me?
There is no Majesdane, Karolina Dean, and I am not a soldier.
I am referring to the survivors. And it's hard to tell civilian from soldier when they're both shooting at you.
I have no weapons. I believe in truth, not violence.
Geez, you argue like a *girl*, dude! Just answer the freakin' question! ***Soldiers! Here! Attacking us! Why?!***

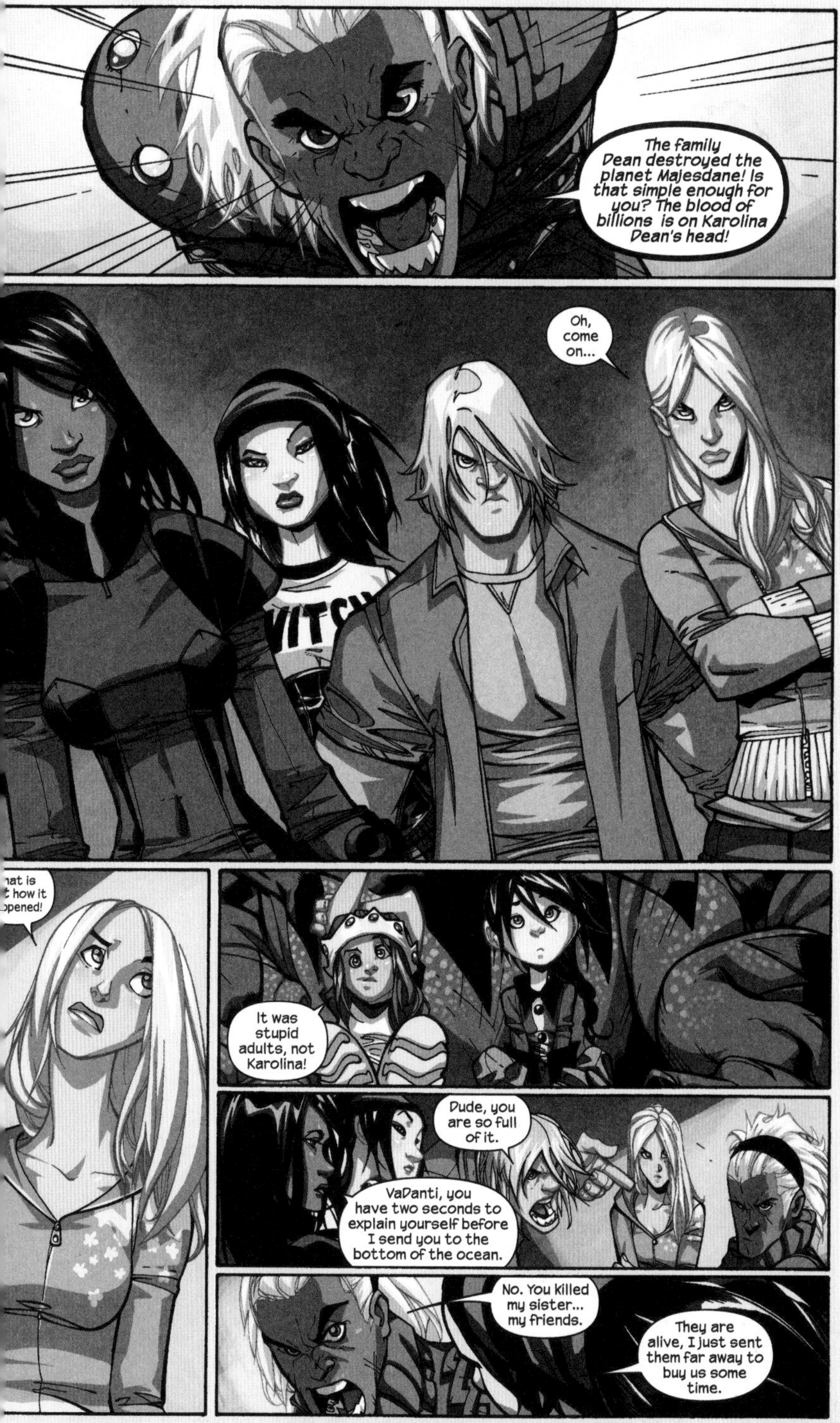
The family Dean destroyed the planet Majesdane! Is that simple enough for you? The blood of billions is on Karolina Dean's head!
Oh, come on...
hat is
t how it
ppened!
It was stupid adults, not Karolina!
Dude, you are so full of it.
VaDanti, you have two seconds to explain yourself before I send you to the bottom of the ocean.
No. You killed my sister... my friends.
They are alive, I just sent them far away to buy us some time.

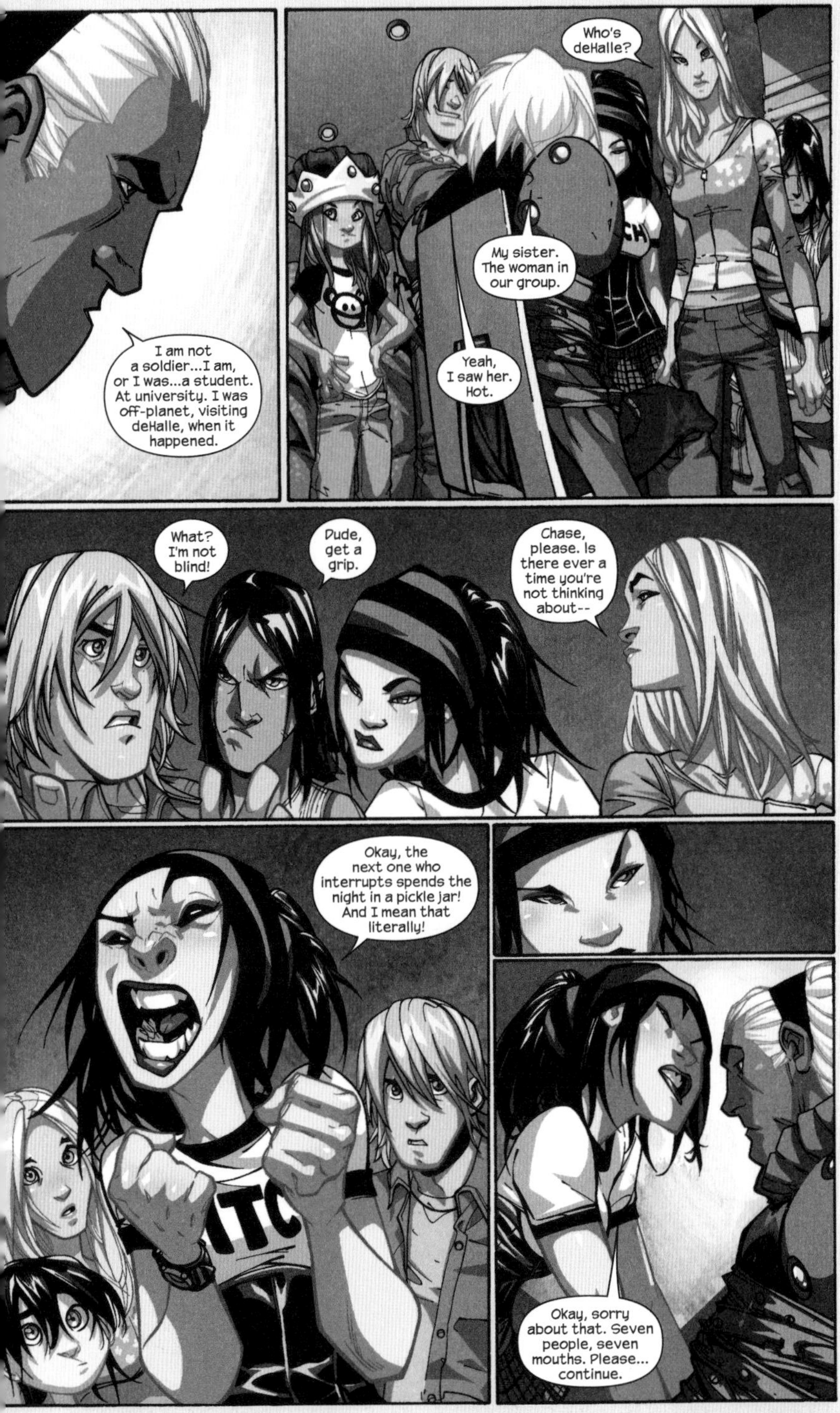

I am not a soldier...I am, or I was...a student. At university. I was off-planet, visiting deHalle, when it happened.
Who's deHalle?
My sister. The woman in our group.
Yeah, I saw her. Hot.
What? I'm not blind!
Dude, get a grip.
Chase, please. Is there ever a time you're not thinking about--
Okay, the next one who interrupts spends the night in a pickle jar! And I mean that literally!
Okay, sorry about that. Seven people, seven mouths. Please... continue.

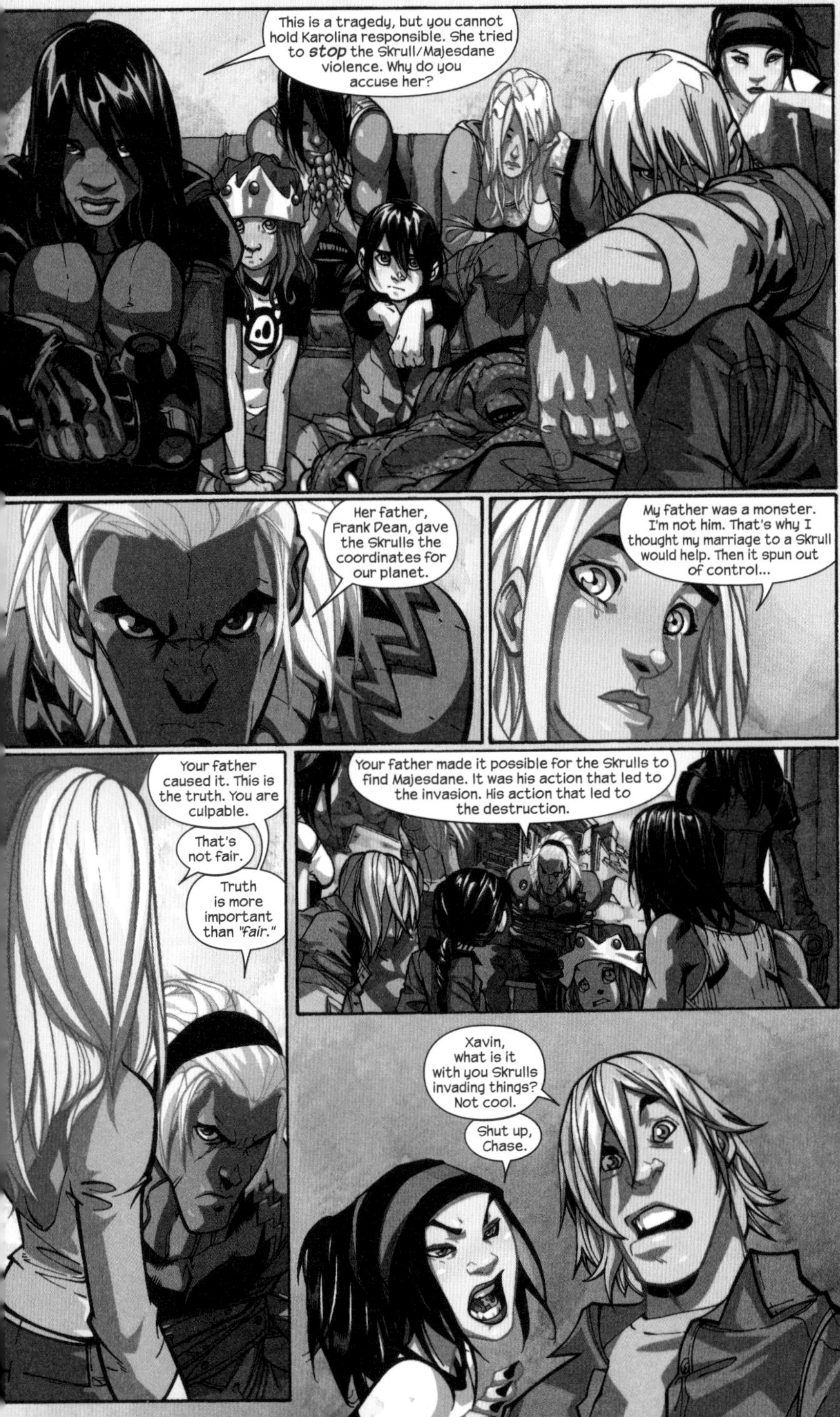

This is a tragedy, but you cannot hold Karolina responsible. She tried to stop the Skrull/Majesdane violence. Why do you accuse her?
Her father, Frank Dean, gave the Skrulls the coordinates for our planet.
My father was a monster. I'm not him. That's why I thought my marriage to a Skrull would help. Then it spun out of control...
Your father caused it. This is the truth. You are culpable.
That's not fair.
Truth is more important than "fair."
Your father made it possible for the Skrulls to find Majesdane. It was his action that led to the invasion. His action that led to the destruction.
Xavin, what is it with you Skrulls invading things? Not cool.
Shut up, Chase.

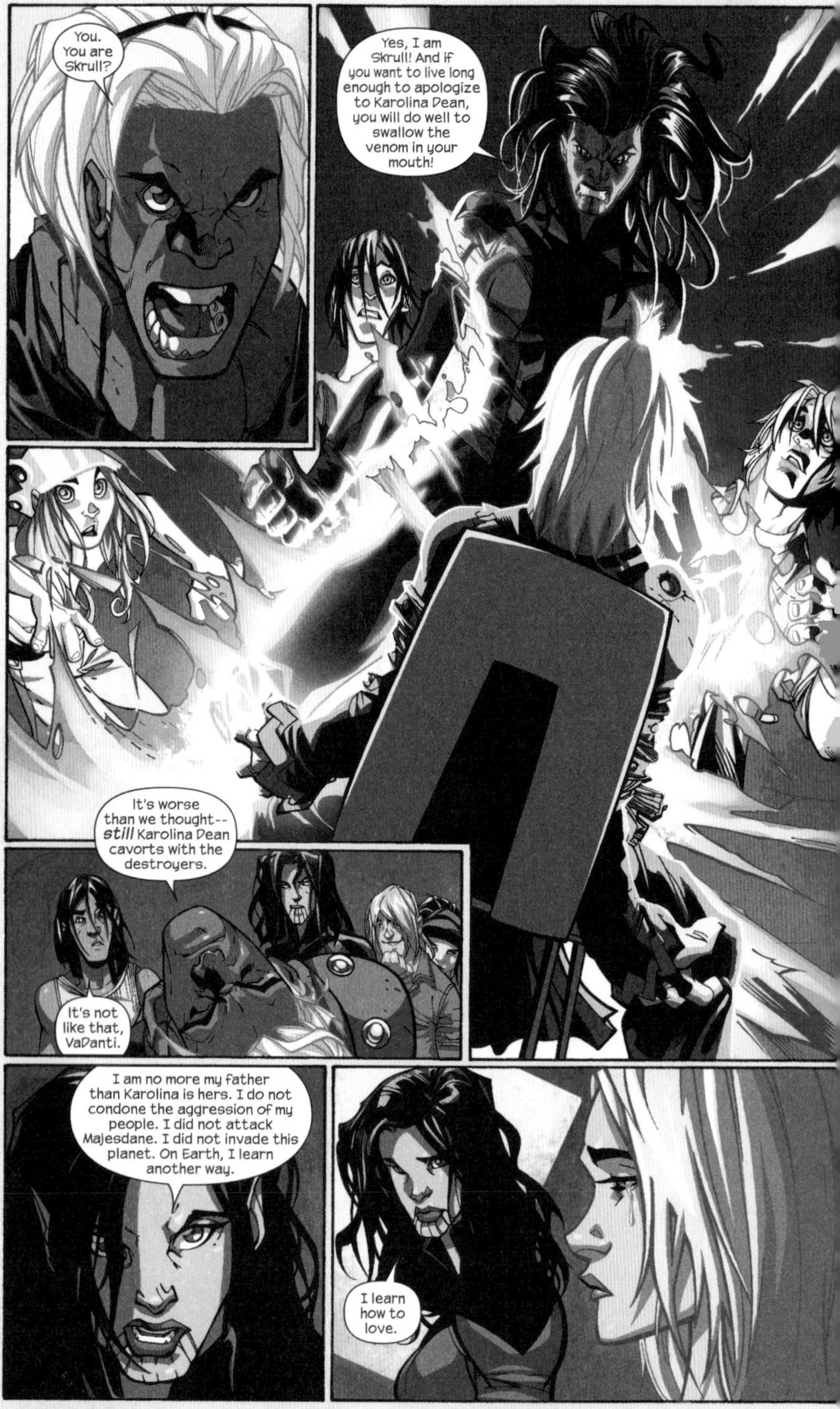

You. You are Skrull?
Yes, I am Skrull! And if you want to live long enough to apologize to Karolina Dean, you will do well to swallow the venom in your mouth!
It's worse than we thought-- *still* Karolina Dean cavorts with the destroyers.
It's not like that, VaDanti.
I am no more my father than Karolina is hers. I do not condone the aggression of my people. I did not attack Majesdane. I did not invade this planet. On Earth, I learn another way.
I learn how to love.

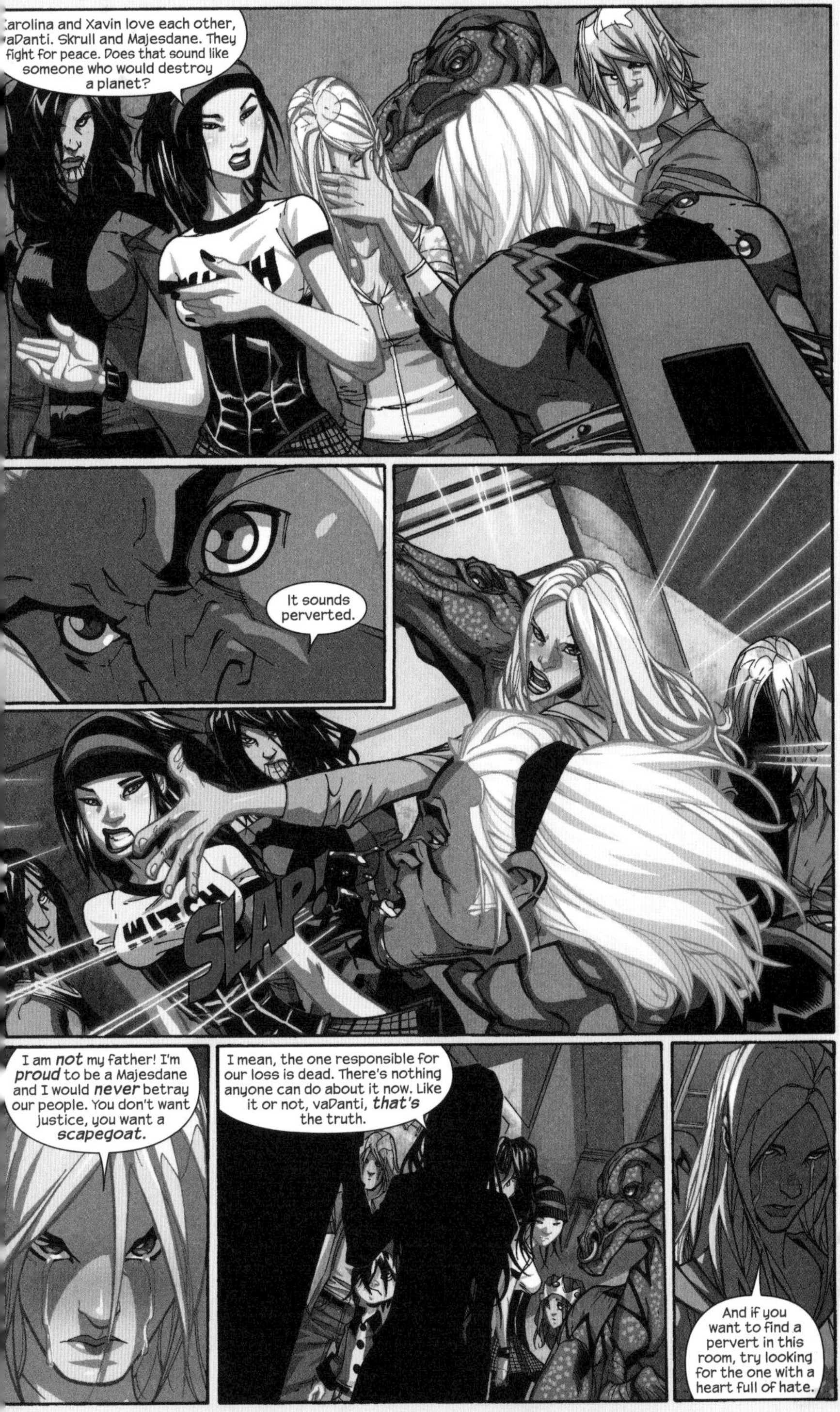

Karolina and Xavin love each other, vaDanti. Skrull and Majesdane. They fight for peace. Does that sound like someone who would destroy a planet?
It sounds perverted.
WITCH
SLAP!
I am not my father! I'm proud to be a Majesdane and I would never betray our people. You don't want justice, you want a scapegoat.
I mean, the one responsible for our loss is dead. There's nothing anyone can do about it now. Like it or not, vaDanti, that's the truth.
And if you want to find a pervert in this room, try looking for the one with a heart full of hate.

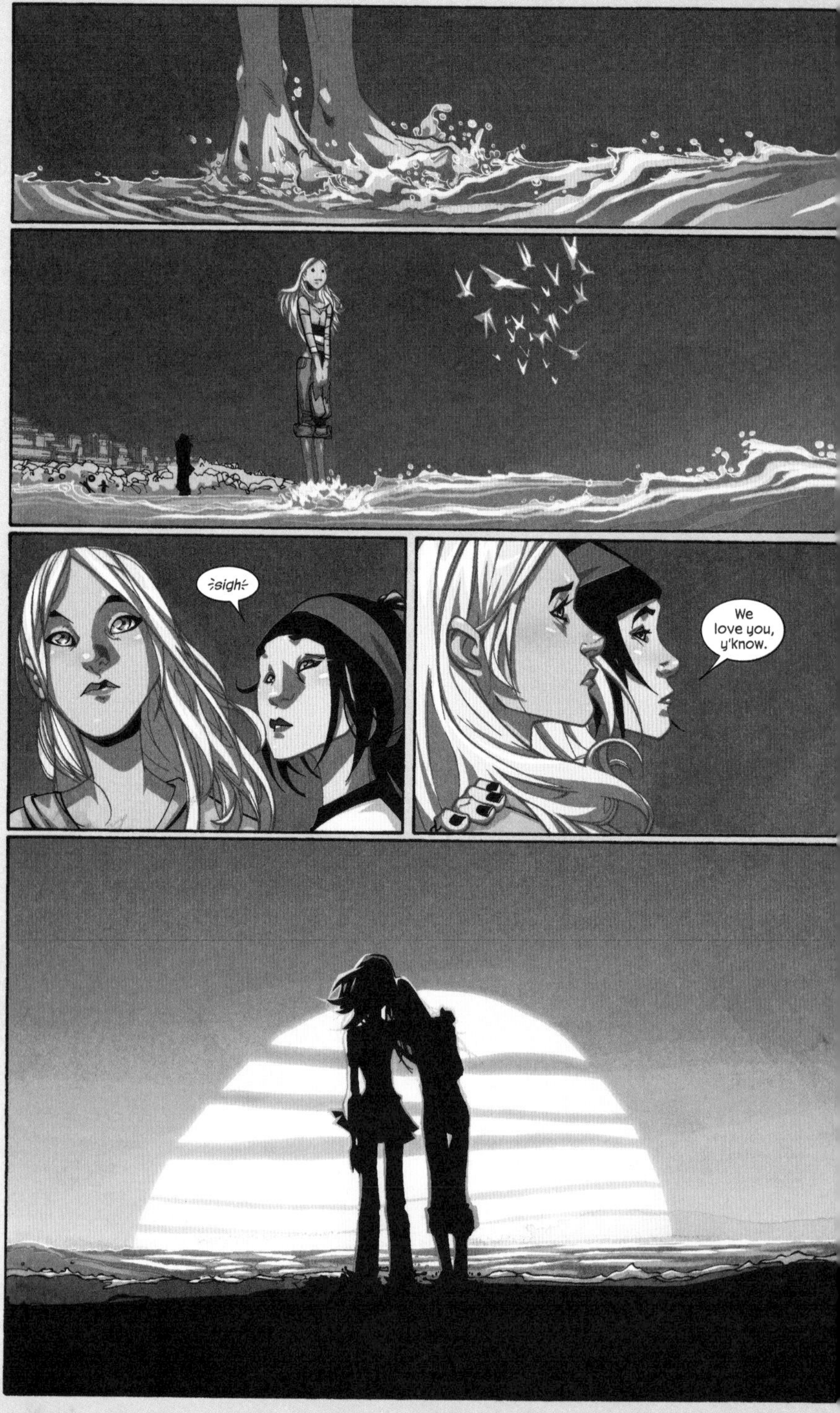

sigh
We love you, y'know.

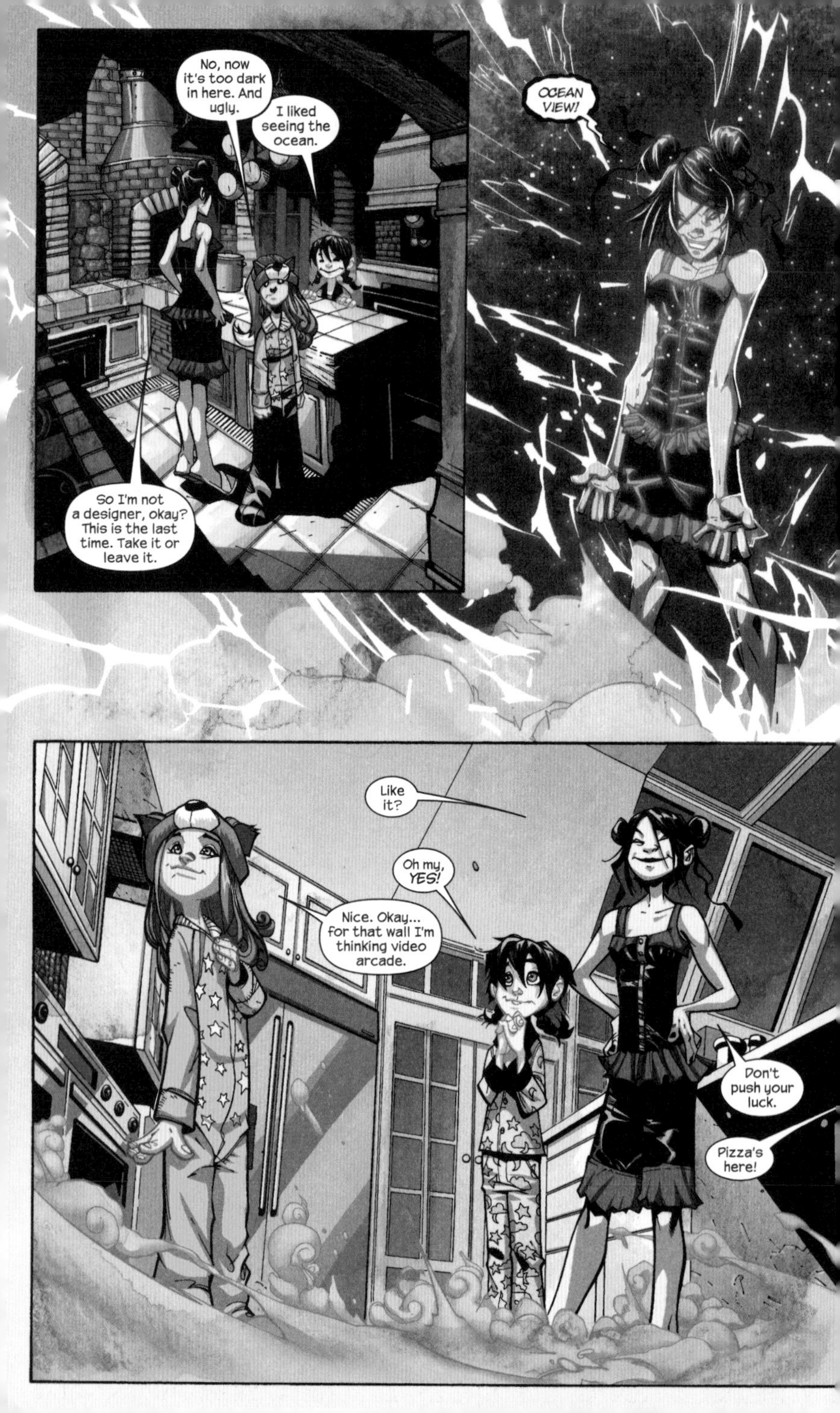
No, now it's too dark in here. And ugly.
I liked seeing the ocean.
So I'm not a designer, okay? This is the last time. Take it or leave it.
OCEAN VIEW!
Like it?
Oh my, YES!
Nice. Okay... for that wall I'm thinking video arcade.
Don't push your luck.
Pizza's here!

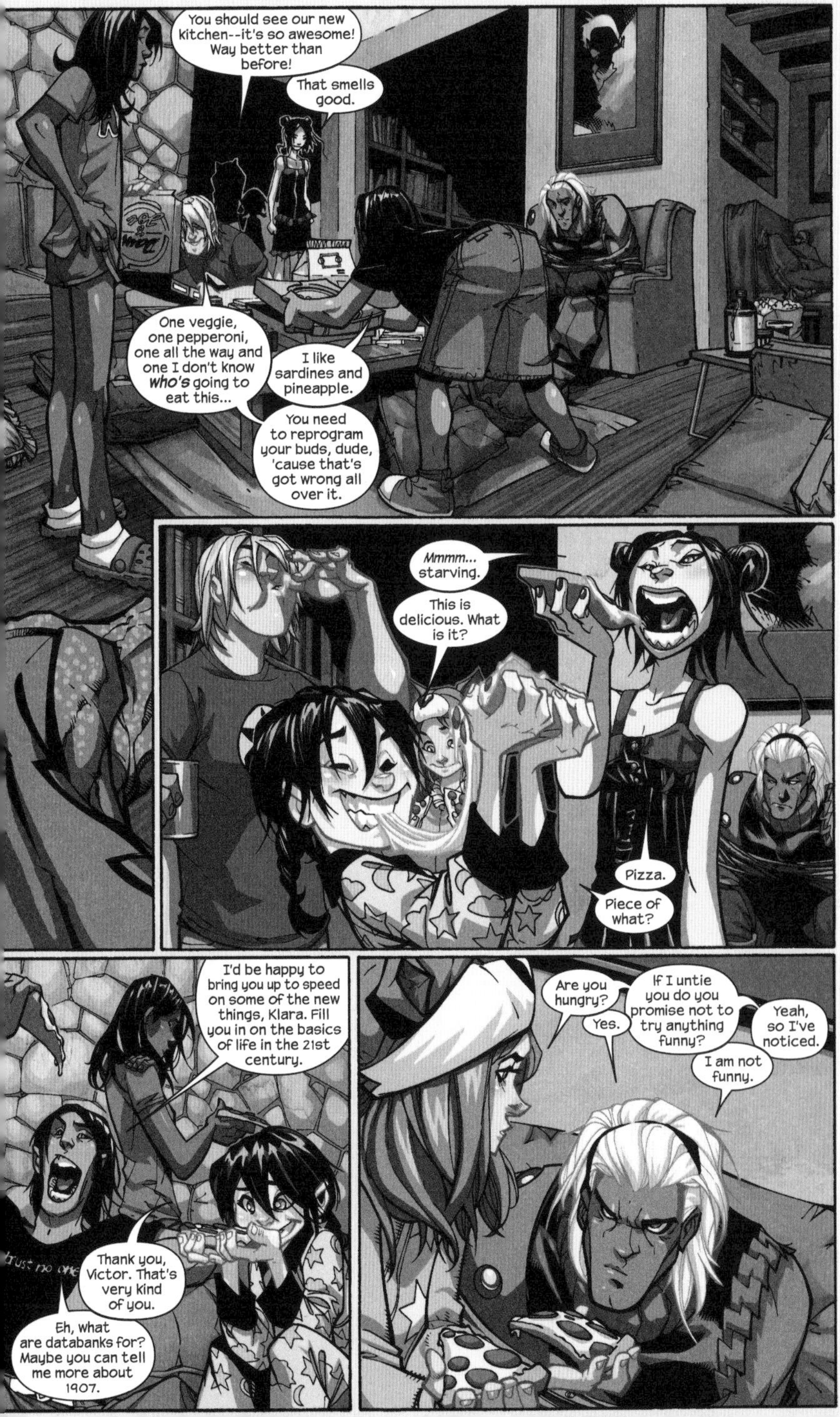

You should see our new kitchen--it's so awesome! Way better than before!
That smells good.
One veggie, one pepperoni, one all the way and one I don't know *who's* going to eat this...
I like sardines and pineapple.
You need to reprogram your buds, dude, 'cause that's got wrong all over it.
Mmmm... starving.
This is delicious. What is it?
Pizza.
Piece of what?
I'd be happy to bring you up to speed on some of the new things, Klara. Fill you in on the basics of life in the 21st century.
Thank you, Victor. That's very kind of you.
Eh, what are databanks for? Maybe you can tell me more about 1907.
trust no one
Are you hungry?
Yes.
If I untie you do you promise not to try anything funny?
I am not funny.
Yeah, so I've noticed.

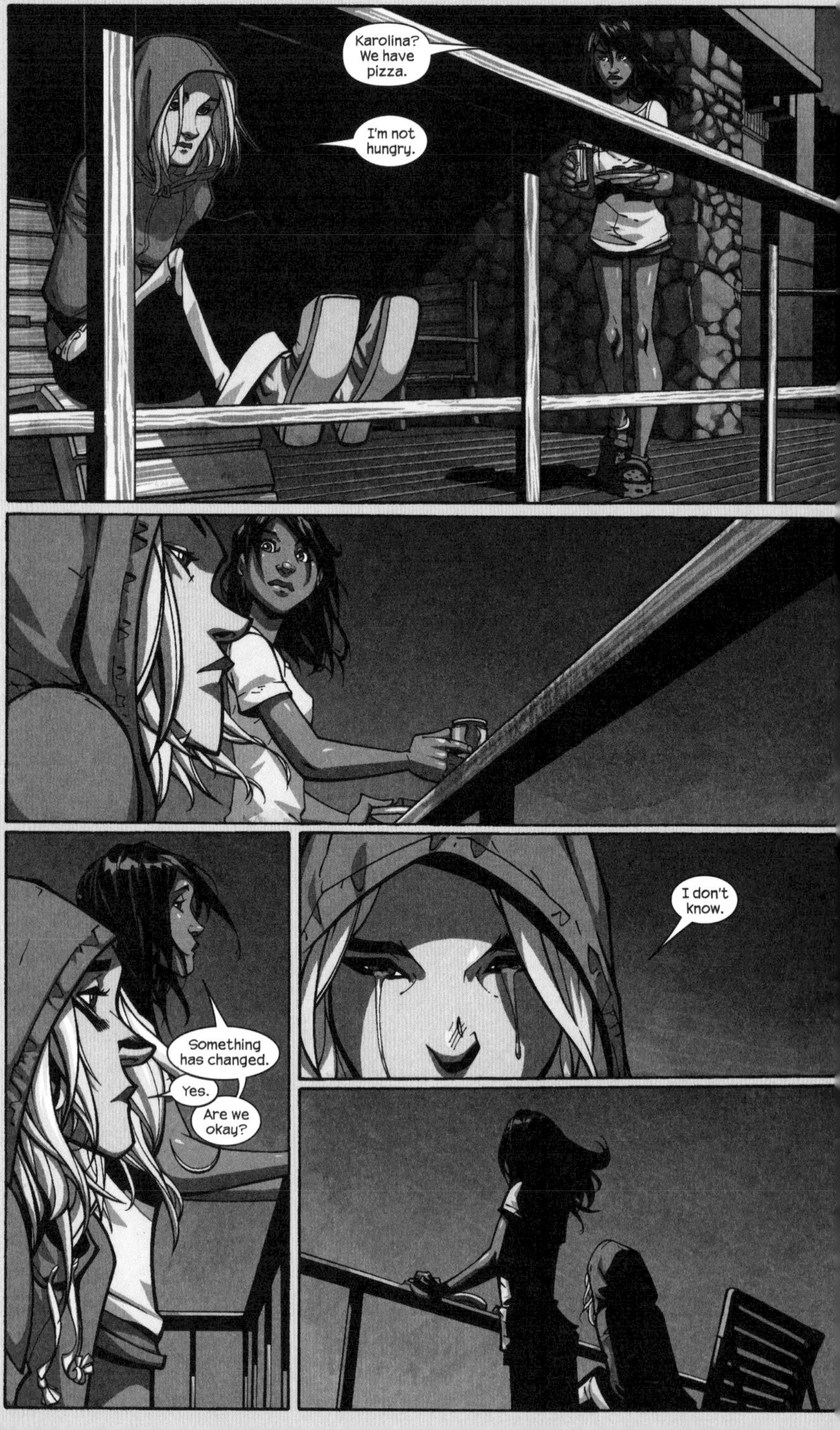
Karolina? We have pizza.
I'm not hungry.
Something has changed.
Yes.
Are we okay?
I don't know.

3

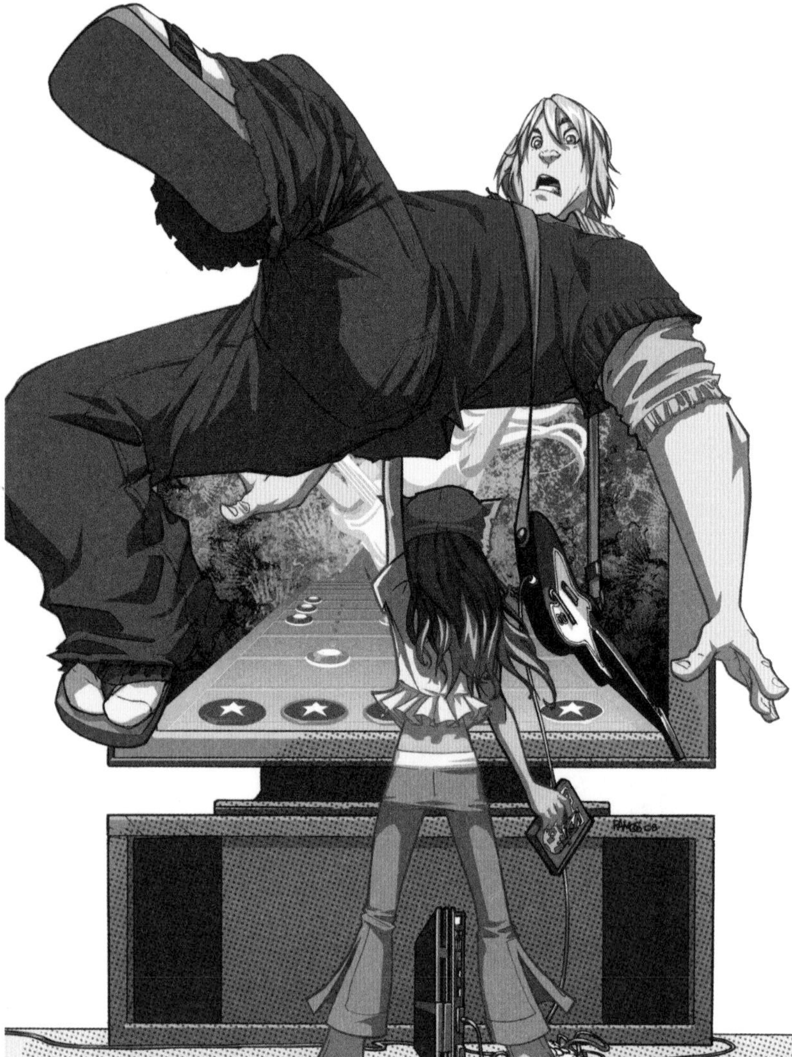

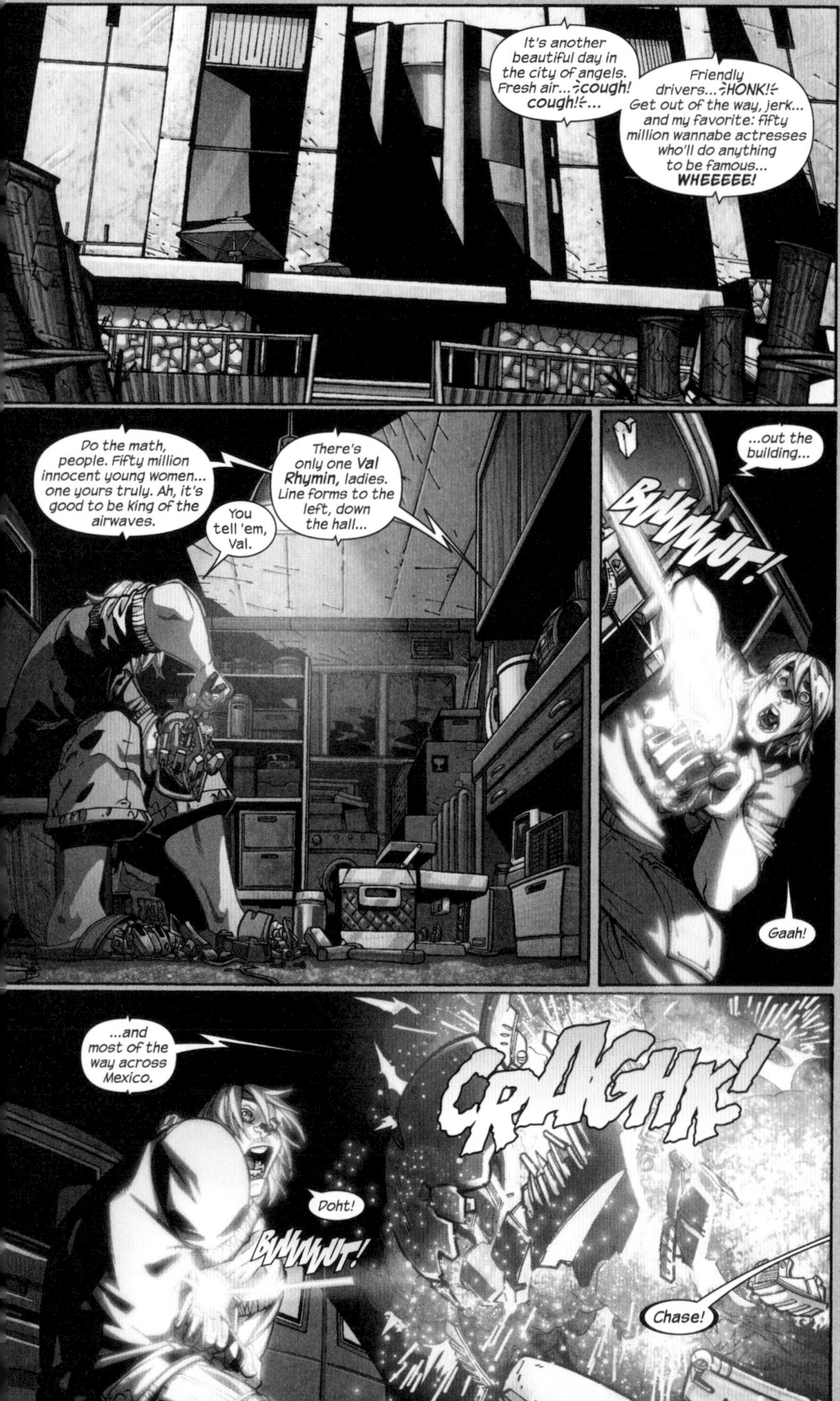
It's another beautiful day in the city of angels. Fresh air... cough! cough!...
Friendly drivers... HONK! Get out of the way, jerk... and my favorite: fifty million wannabe actresses who'll do anything to be famous... WHEEEEE!
Do the math, people. Fifty million innocent young women... one yours truly. Ah, it's good to be king of the airwaves.
You tell 'em, Val.
There's only one Val Rhymin, ladies. Line forms to the left, down the hall...
...out the building...
BWWWUT!
Gaah!
...and most of the way across Mexico.
CRACHK!
Doht!
BWWWUT!
Chase!

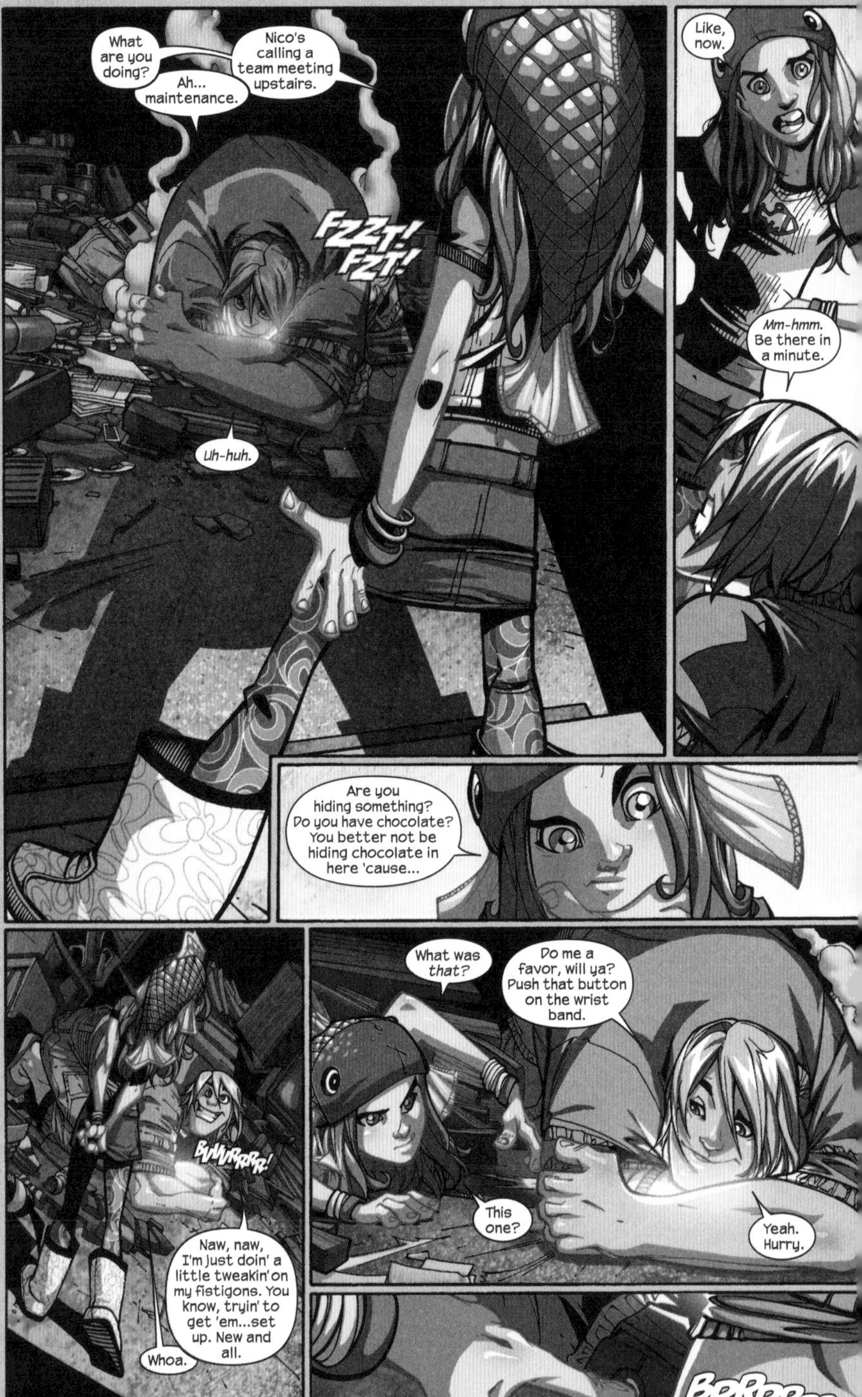
What are you doing?
Nico's calling a team meeting upstairs.
Ah... maintenance.
FZZT! FZT!
Uh-huh.
Like, now.
Mm-hmm. Be there in a minute.
Are you hiding something? Do you have chocolate? You better not be hiding chocolate in here 'cause...
BWWRRRR!
Naw, naw, I'm just doin' a little tweakin' on my fistigons. You know, tryin' to get 'em...set up. New and all.
Whoa.
What was that?
Do me a favor, will ya? Push that button on the wrist band.
This one?
Yeah. Hurry.
BRRRRRRRR...

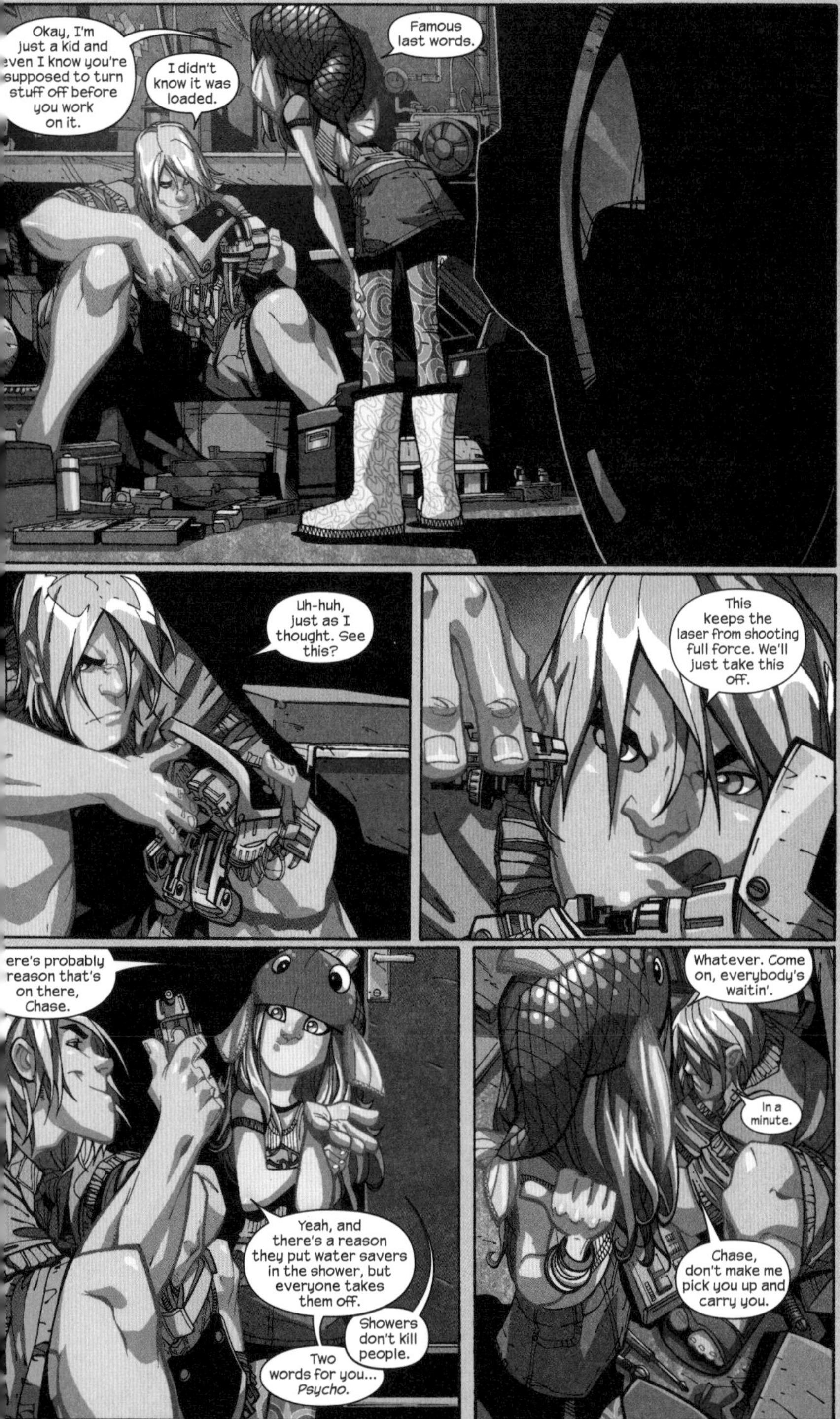
Okay, I'm
just a kid and
even I know you're
supposed to turn
stuff off before
you work
on it.
I didn't
know it was
loaded.
Famous
last words.
Uh-huh,
just as I
thought. See
this?
This
keeps the
laser from shooting
full force. We'll
just take this
off.
ere's probably
reason that's
on there,
Chase.
Yeah, and
there's a reason
they put water savers
in the shower, but
everyone takes
them off.
Showers
don't kill
people.
Two
words for you...
Psycho.
Whatever. Come
on, everybody's
waitin'.
In a
minute.
Chase,
don't make me
pick you up and
carry you.

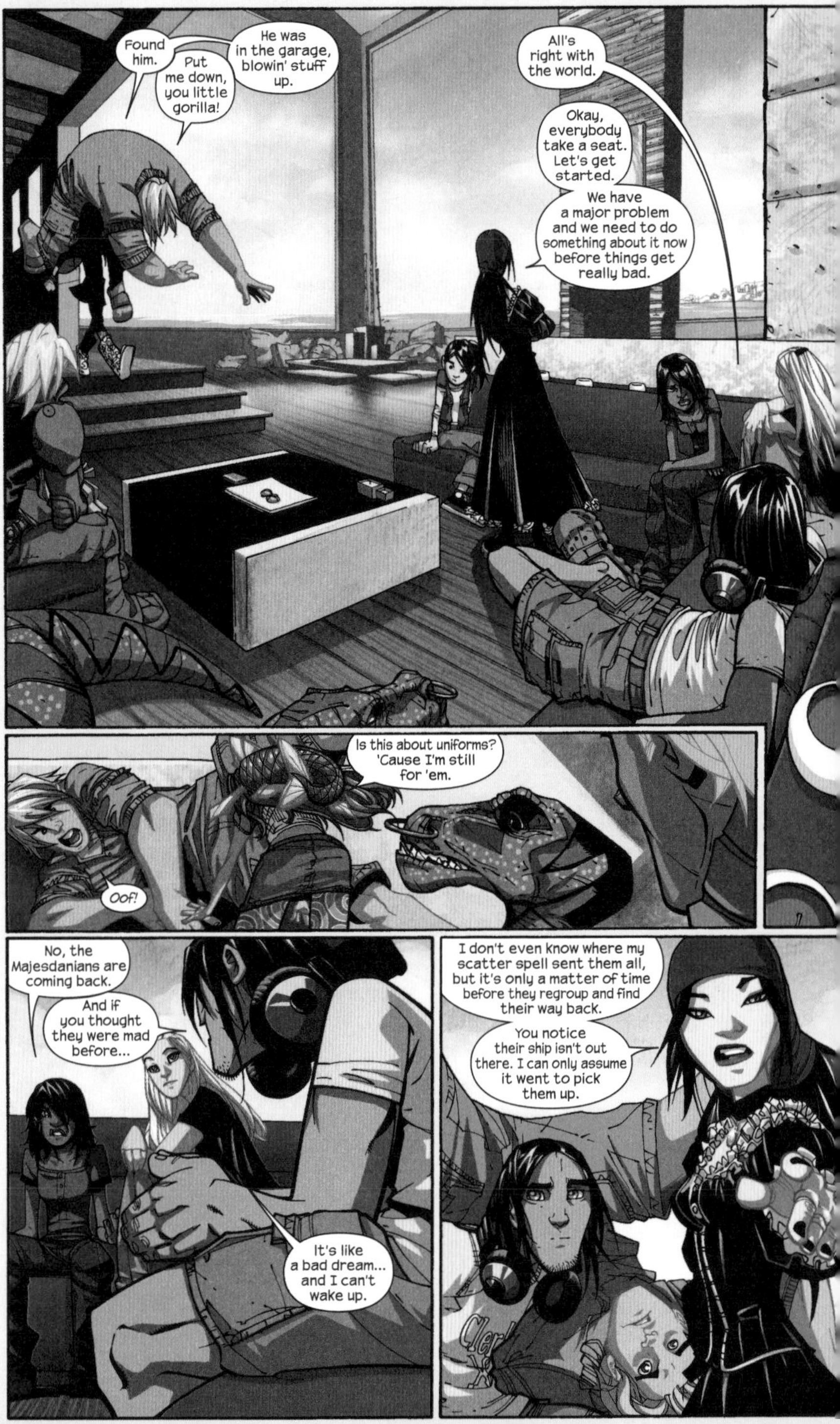
Found him.
He was in the garage, blowin' stuff up.
Put me down, you little gorilla!
All's right with the world.
Okay, everybody take a seat. Let's get started.
We have a major problem and we need to do something about it now before things get really bad.
Is this about uniforms? 'Cause I'm still for 'em.
Oof!
No, the Majesdanians are coming back.
And if you thought they were mad before...
It's like a bad dream... and I can't wake up.
I don't even know where my scatter spell sent them all, but it's only a matter of time before they regroup and find their way back.
You notice their ship isn't out there. I can only assume it went to pick them up.

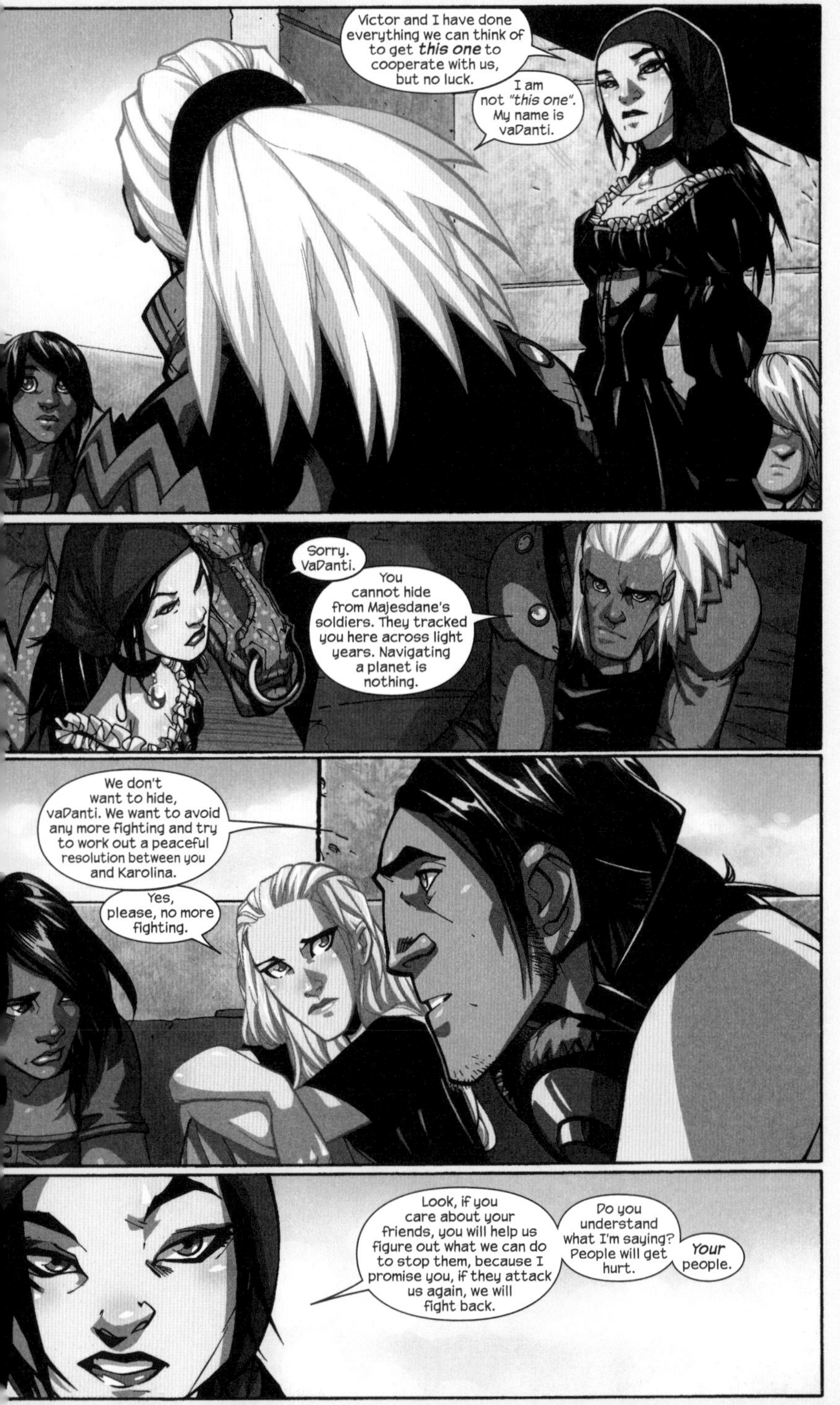

Victor and I have done everything we can think of to get *this one* to cooperate with us, but no luck.
I am not "*this one*". My name is vaDanti.
Sorry. VaDanti.
You cannot hide from Majesdane's soldiers. They tracked you here across light years. Navigating a planet is nothing.
We don't want to hide, vaDanti. We want to avoid any more fighting and try to work out a peaceful resolution between you and Karolina.
Yes, please, no more fighting.
Look, if you care about your friends, you will help us figure out what we can do to stop them, because I promise you, if they attack us again, we will fight back.
Do you understand what I'm saying? People will get hurt.
Your people.

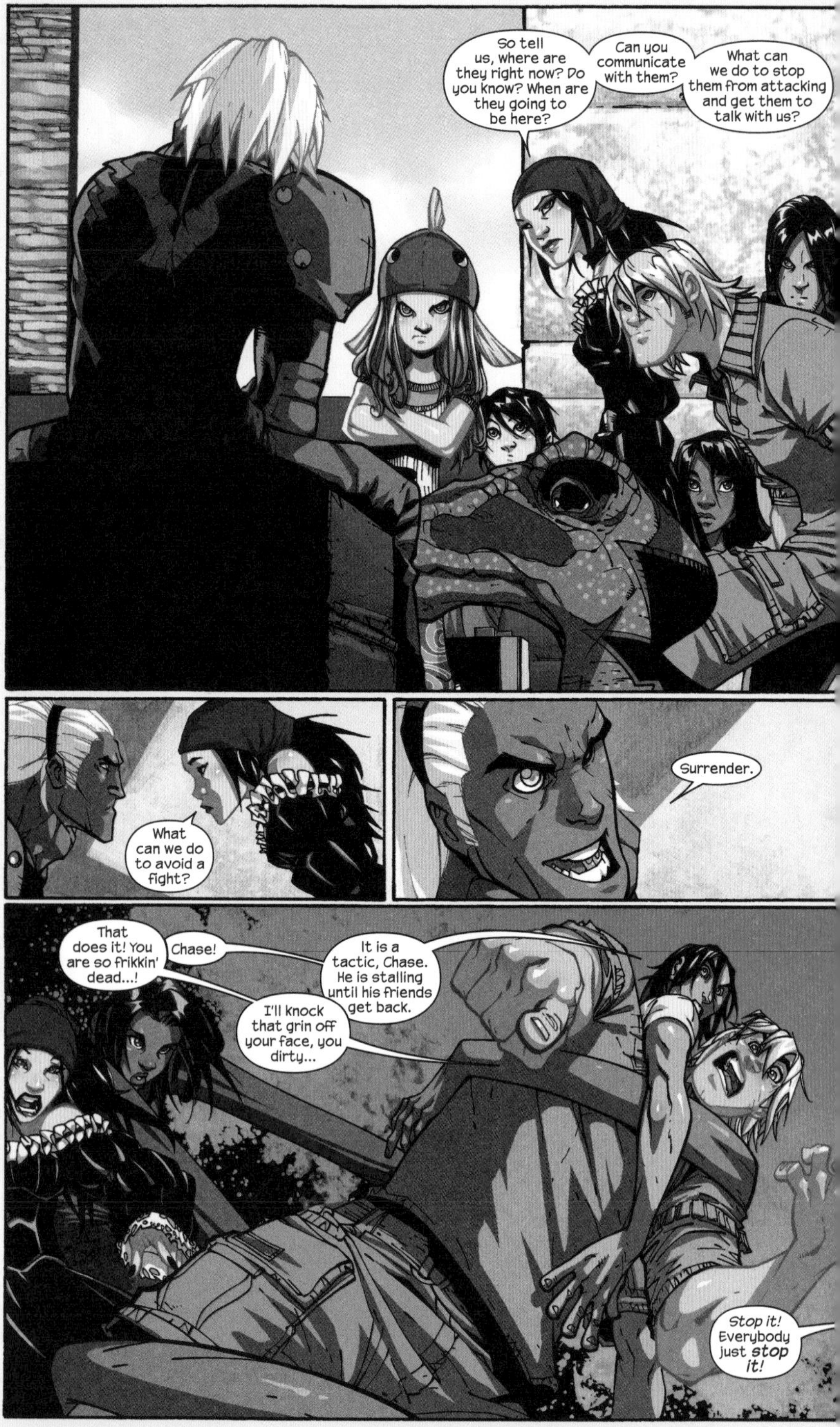

So tell us, where are they right now? Do you know? When are they going to be here?
Can you communicate with them?
What can we do to stop them from attacking and get them to talk with us?
What can we do to avoid a fight?
Surrender.
That does it! You are so frikkin' dead...!
Chase!
It is a tactic, Chase. He is stalling until his friends get back.
I'll knock that grin off your face, you dirty...
Stop it! Everybody just *stop it!*

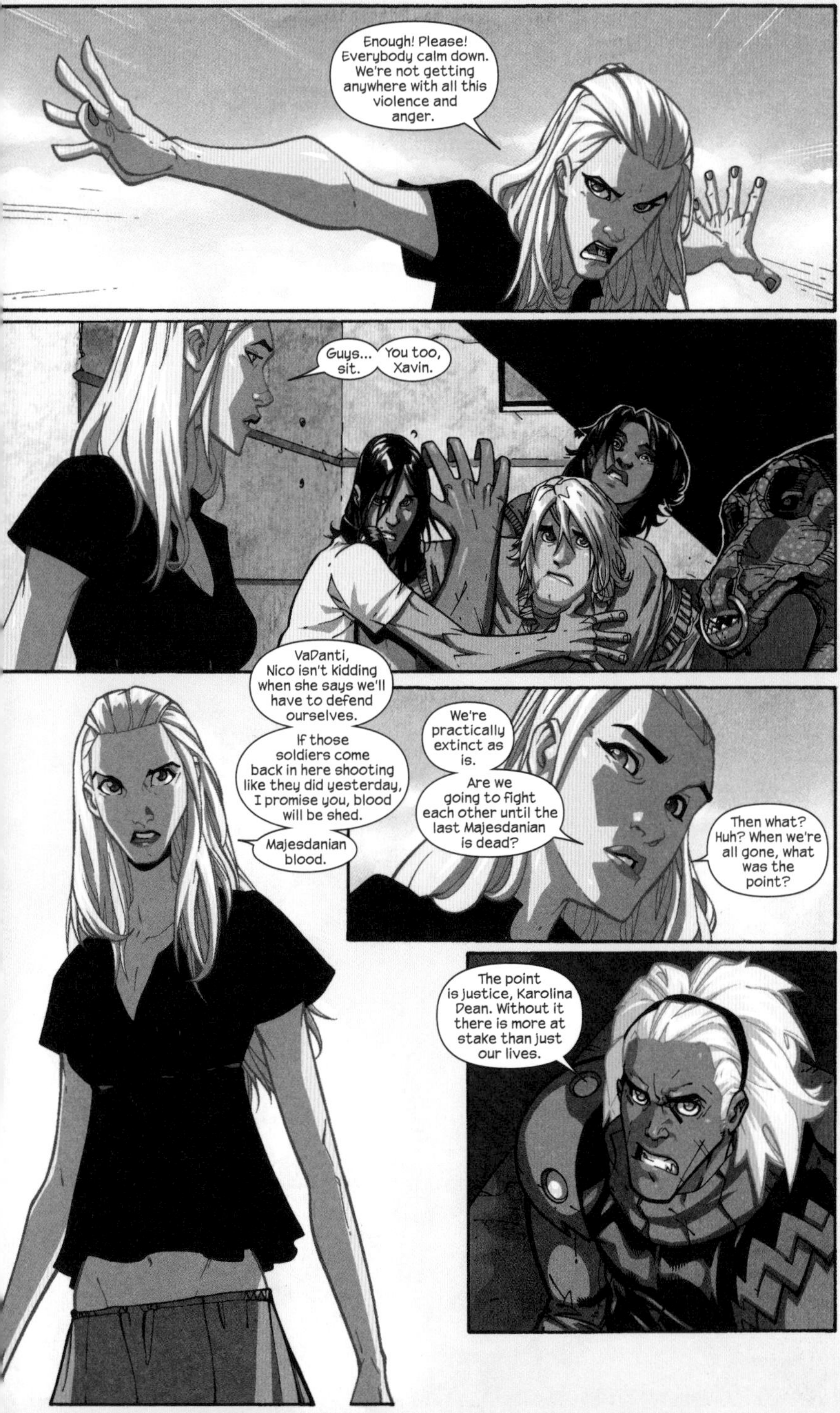
Enough! Please! Everybody calm down. We're not getting anywhere with all this violence and anger.
Guys... sit.
You too, Xavin.
VaDanti, Nico isn't kidding when she says we'll have to defend ourselves.
If those soldiers come back in here shooting like they did yesterday, I promise you, blood will be shed.
Majesdanian blood.
We're practically extinct as is.
Are we going to fight each other until the last Majesdanian is dead?
Then what? Huh? When we're all gone, what was the point?
The point is justice, Karolina Dean. Without it there is more at stake than just our lives.

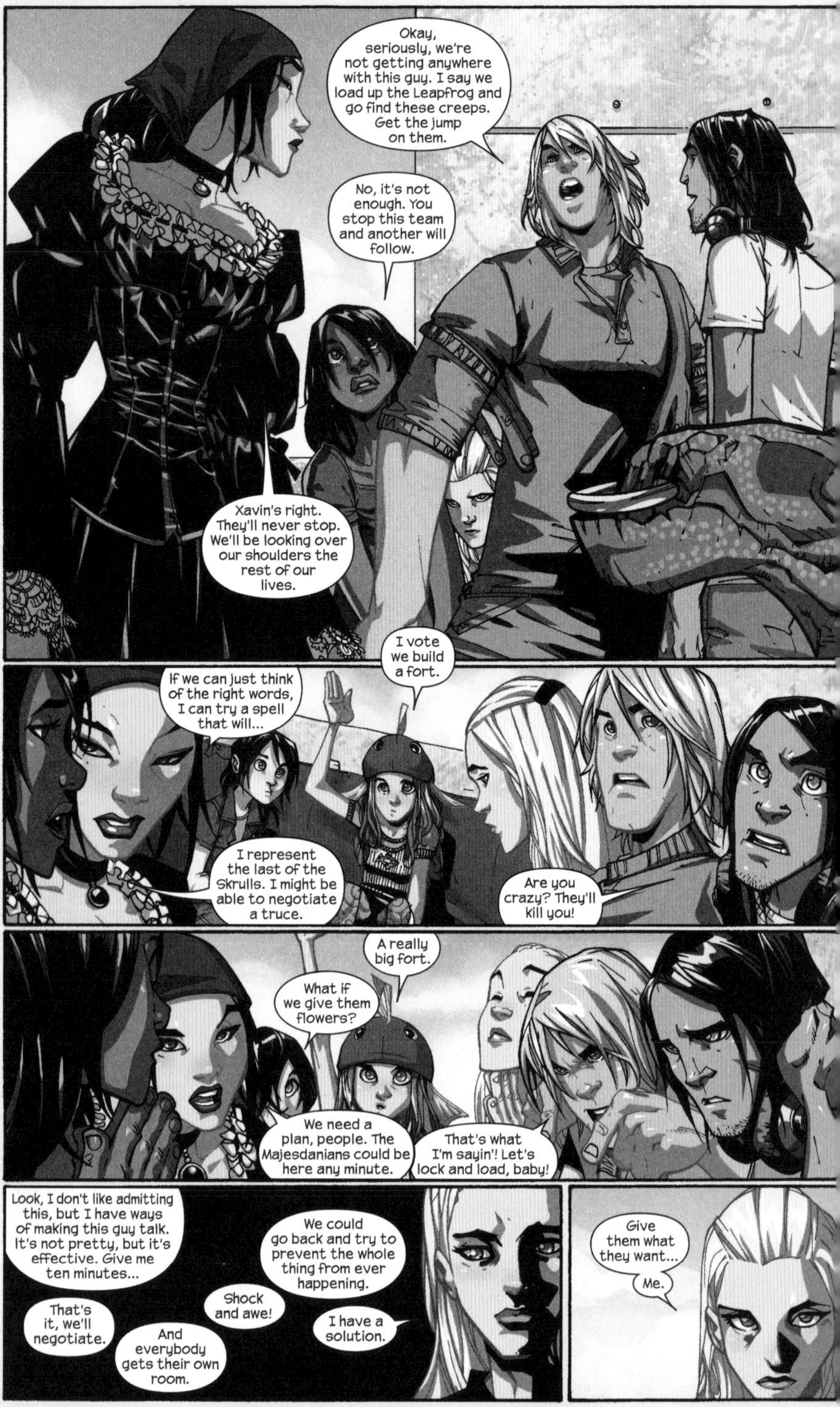

Okay, seriously, we're not getting anywhere with this guy. I say we load up the Leapfrog and go find these creeps. Get the jump on them.
No, it's not enough. You stop this team and another will follow.
Xavin's right. They'll never stop. We'll be looking over our shoulders the rest of our lives.
If we can just think of the right words, I can try a spell that will...
I vote we build a fort.
I represent the last of the Skrulls. I might be able to negotiate a truce.
Are you crazy? They'll kill you!
A really big fort.
What if we give them flowers?
We need a plan, people. The Majesdanians could be here any minute.
That's what I'm sayin'! Let's lock and load, baby!
Look, I don't like admitting this, but I have ways of making this guy talk. It's not pretty, but it's effective. Give me ten minutes...
We could go back and try to prevent the whole thing from ever happening.
Shock and awe!
That's it, we'll negotiate.
And everybody gets their own room.
I have a solution.
Give them what they want...
Me.

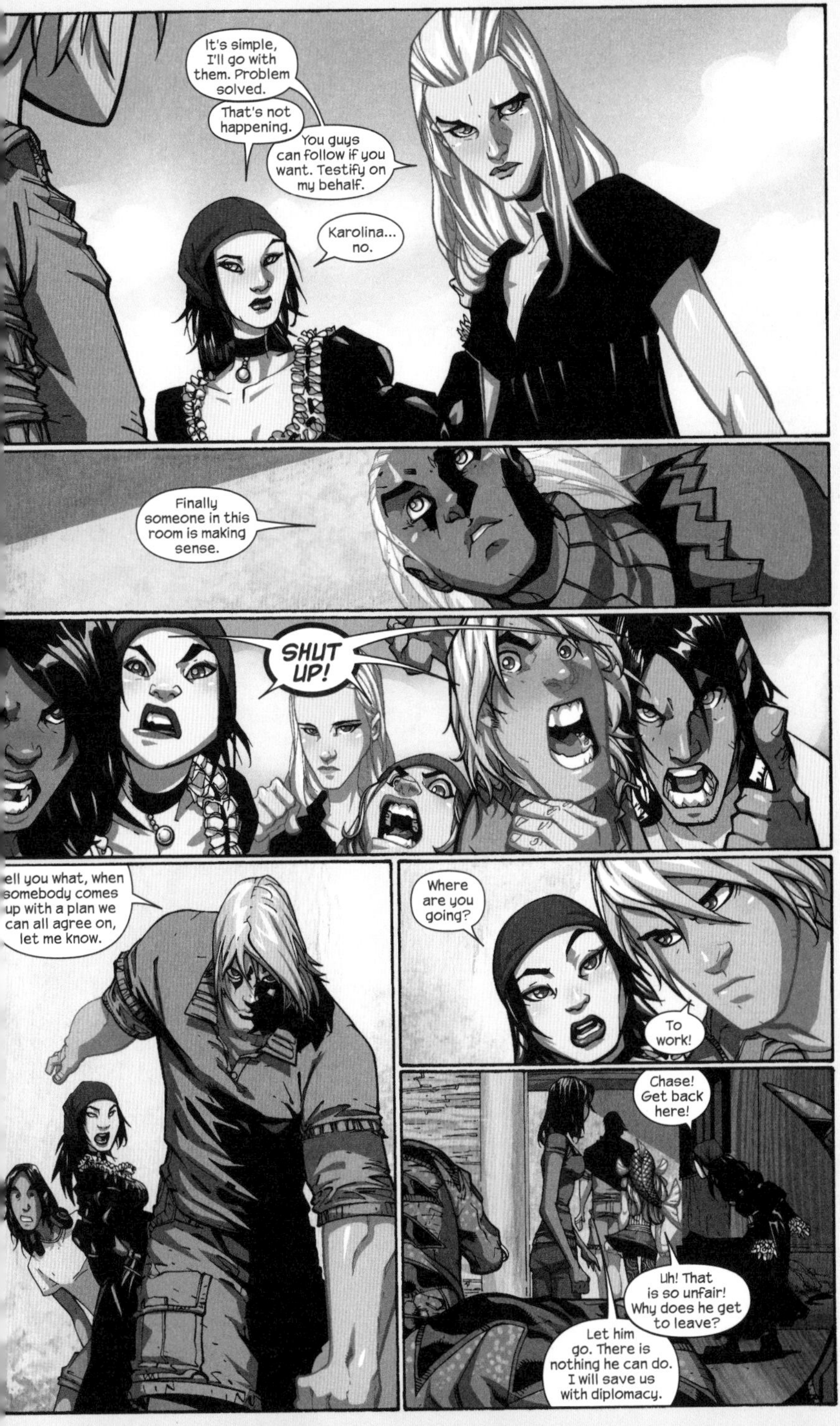
It's simple, I'll go with them. Problem solved.
That's not happening.
You guys can follow if you want. Testify on my behalf.
Karolina... no.
Finally someone in this room is making sense.
SHUT UP!
ell you what, when somebody comes up with a plan we can all agree on, let me know.
Where are you going?
To work!
Chase! Get back here!
Uh! That is so unfair! Why does he get to leave?
Let him go. There is nothing he can do. I will save us with diplomacy.

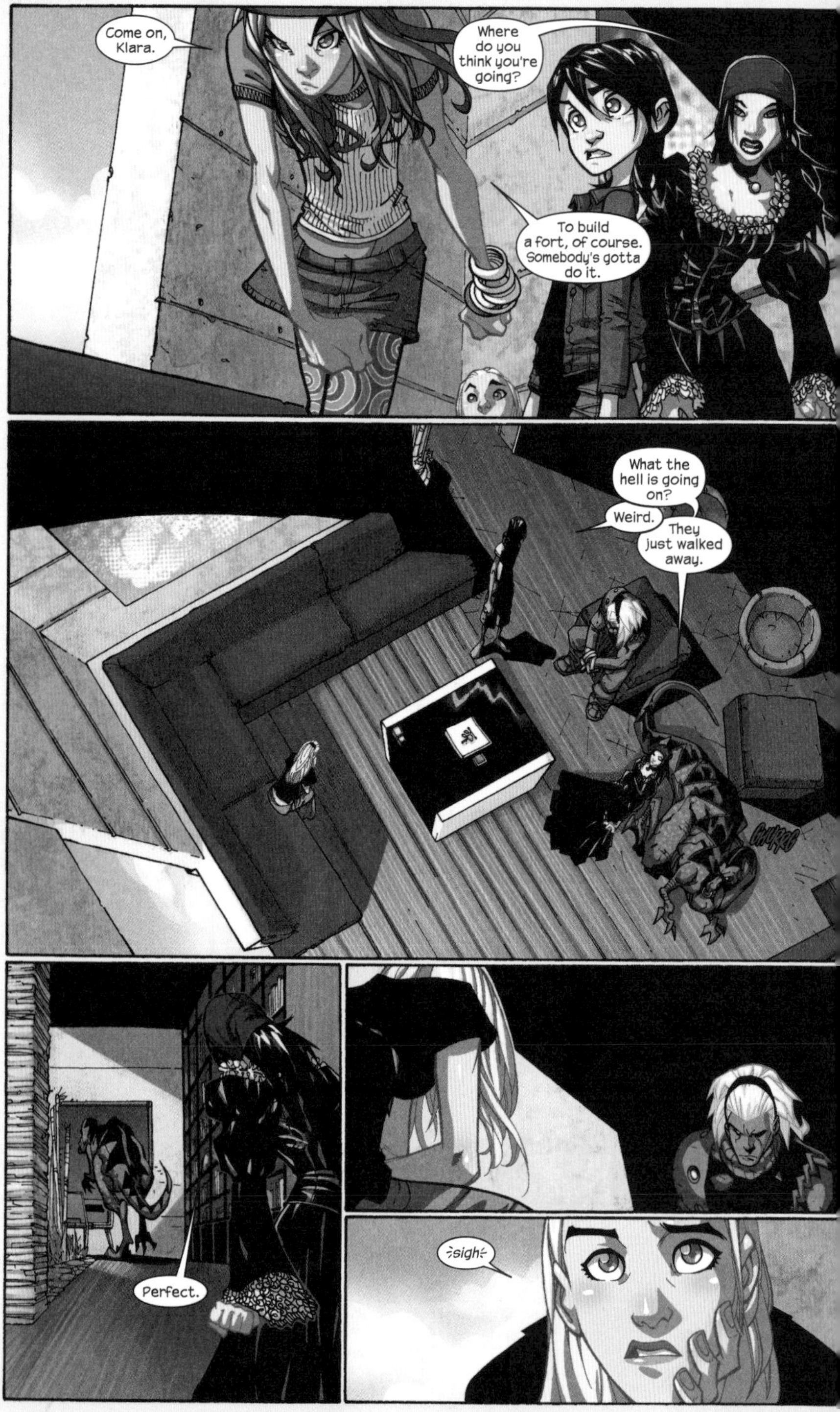
Come on, Klara.
Where do you think you're going?
To build a fort, of course. Somebody's gotta do it.
What the hell is going on?
Weird.
They just walked away.
Perfect.
sigh

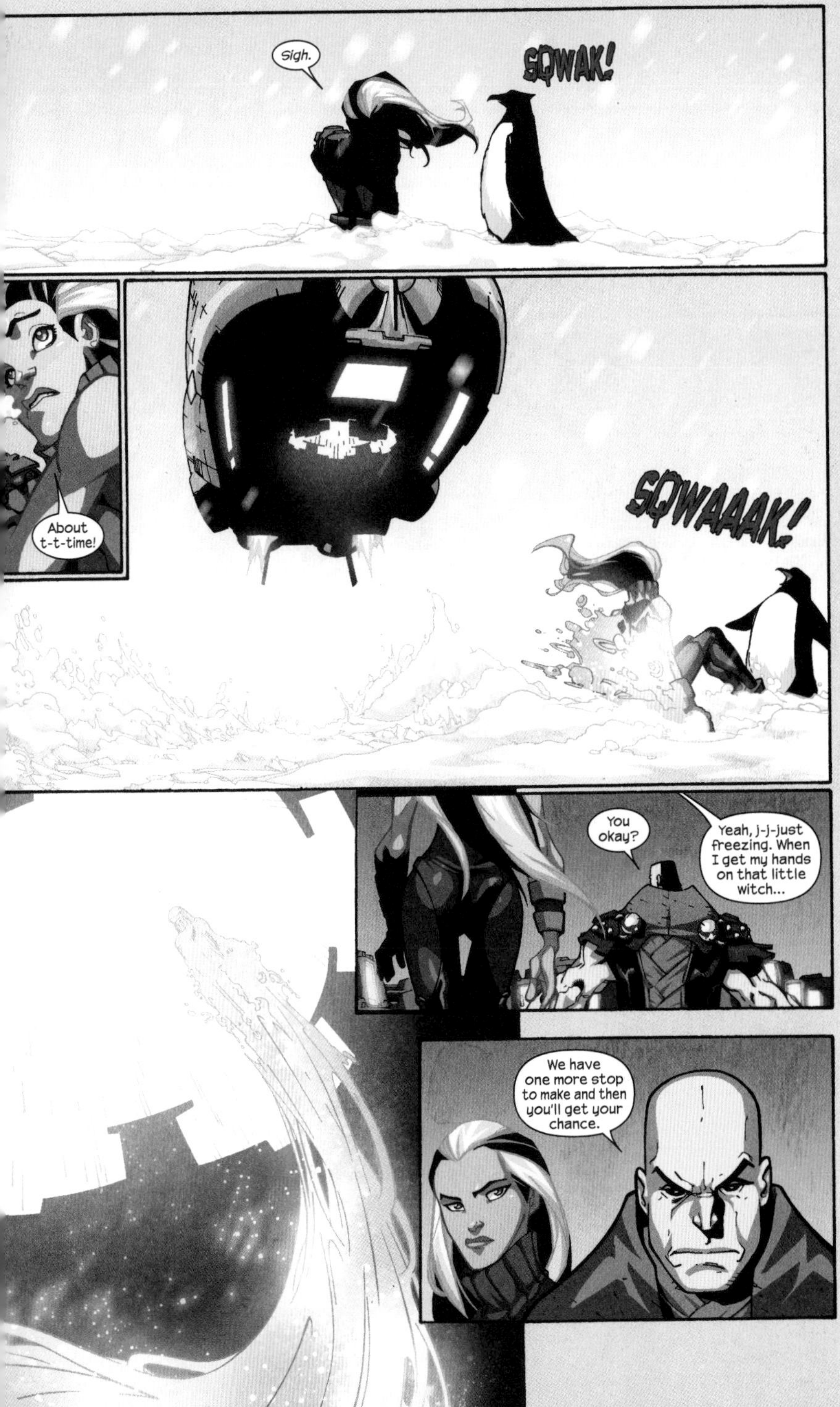
Sigh.
SQWAK!
About t-t-time!
SQWAAAK!
You okay?
Yeah, j-j-just freezing. When I get my hands on that little witch...
We have one more stop to make and then you'll get your chance.

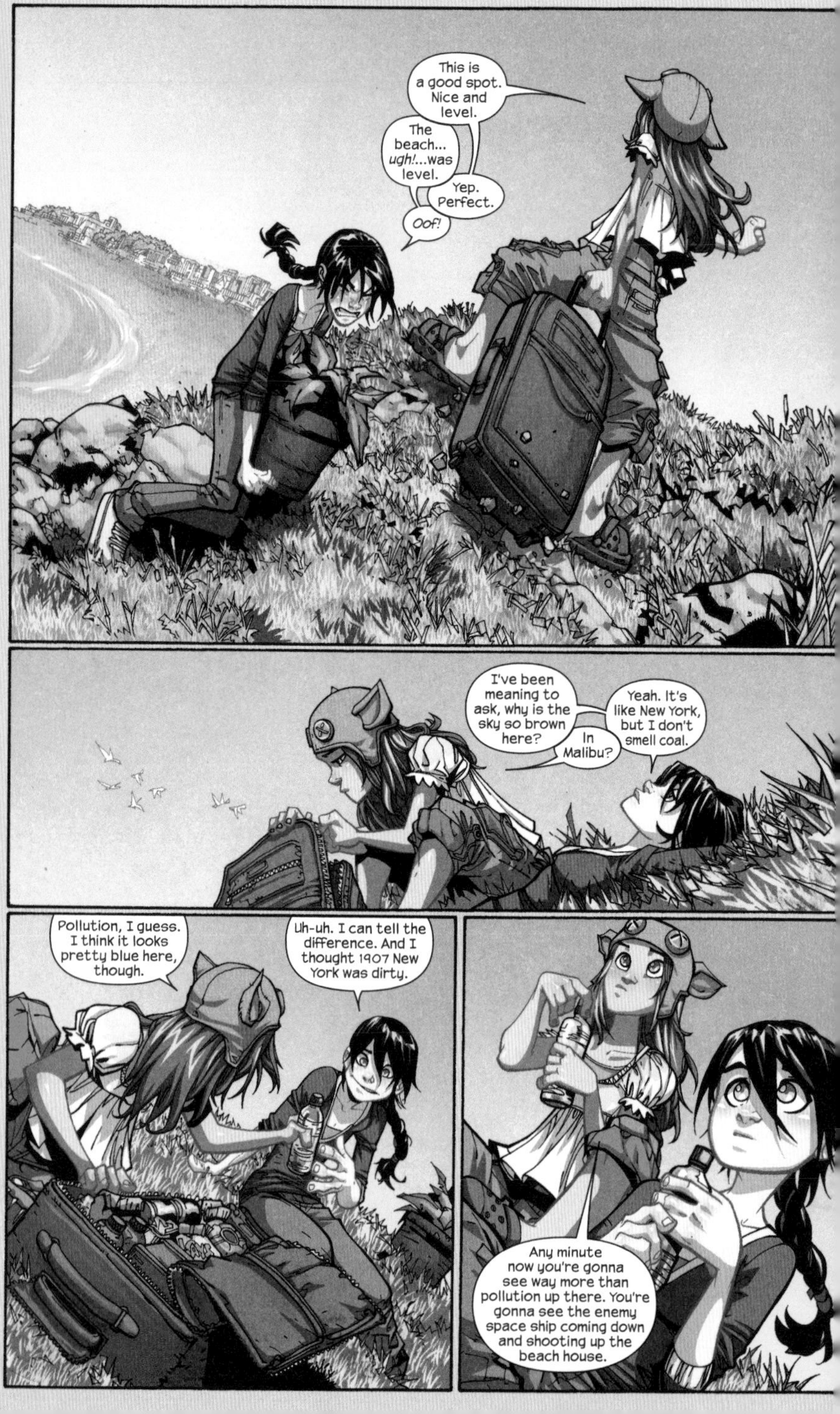
This is a good spot. Nice and level.
The beach... ugh!...was level.
Yep. Perfect.
Oof!
I've been meaning to ask, why is the sky so brown here?
In Malibu?
Yeah. It's like New York, but I don't smell coal.
Pollution, I guess. I think it looks pretty blue here, though.
Uh-uh. I can tell the difference. And I thought 1907 New York was dirty.
Any minute now you're gonna see way more than pollution up there. You're gonna see the enemy space ship coming down and shooting up the beach house.

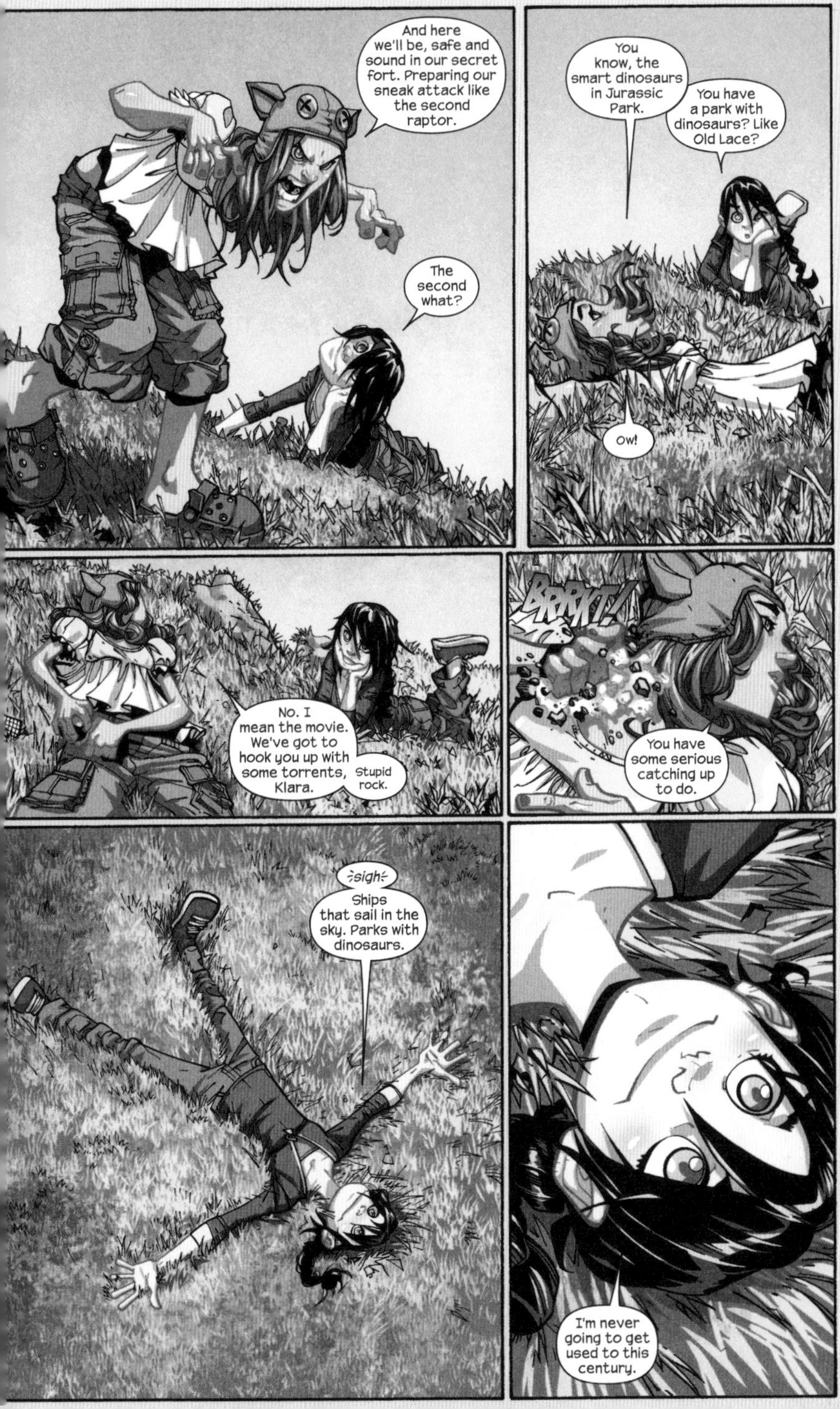

And here we'll be, safe and sound in our secret fort. Preparing our sneak attack like the second raptor.
The second what?
You know, the smart dinosaurs in Jurassic Park.
You have a park with dinosaurs? Like Old Lace?
Ow!
No. I mean the movie. We've got to hook you up with some torrents, Klara.
Stupid rock.
BRRKT!
You have some serious catching up to do.
sigh
Ships that sail in the sky. Parks with dinosaurs.
I'm never going to get used to this century.

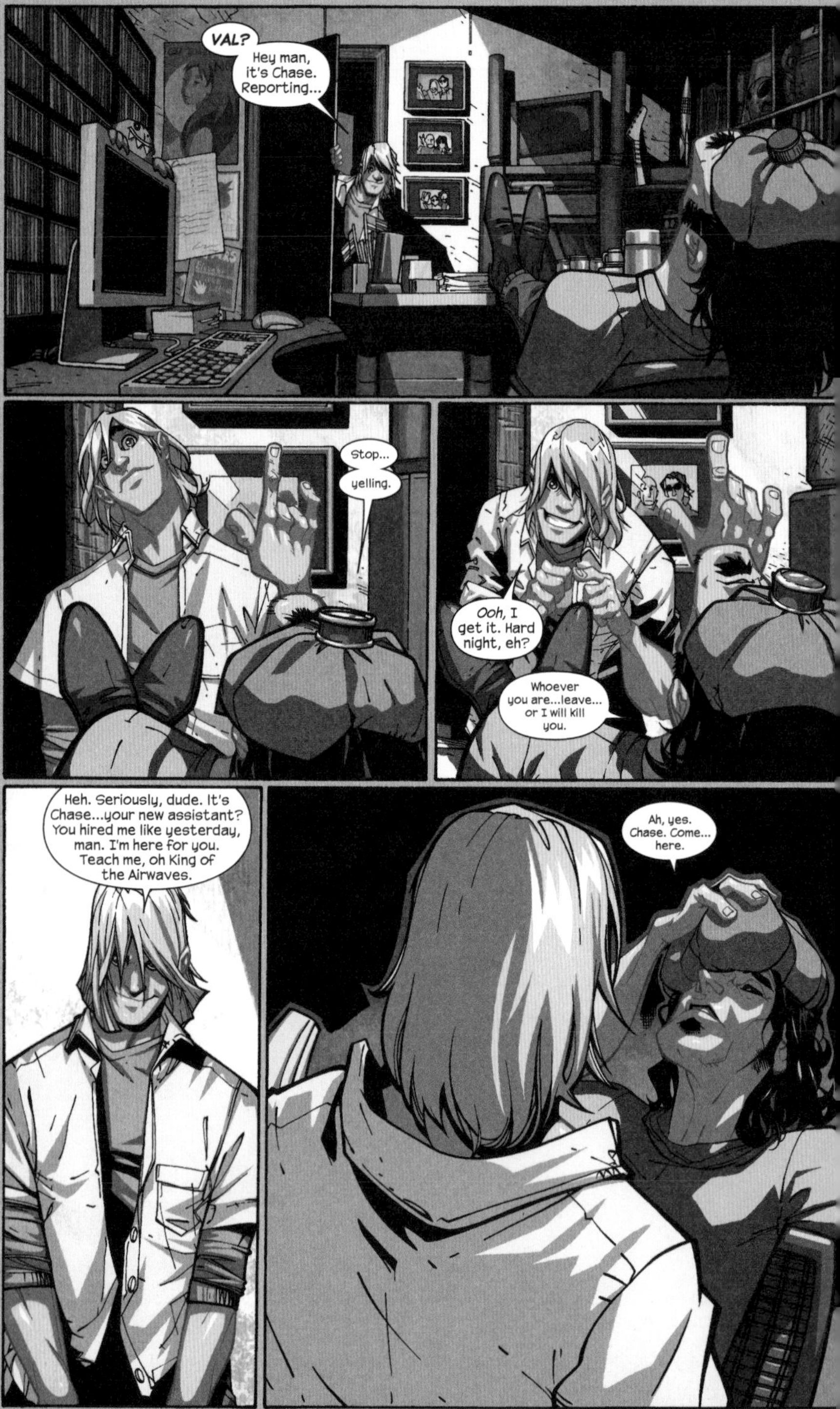
VAL?
Hey man, it's Chase. Reporting...
Stop...
yelling.
Ooh, I get it. Hard night, eh?
Whoever you are...leave... or I will kill you.
Heh. Seriously, dude. It's Chase...your new assistant? You hired me like yesterday, man. I'm here for you. Teach me, oh King of the Airwaves.
Ah, yes. Chase. Come... here.

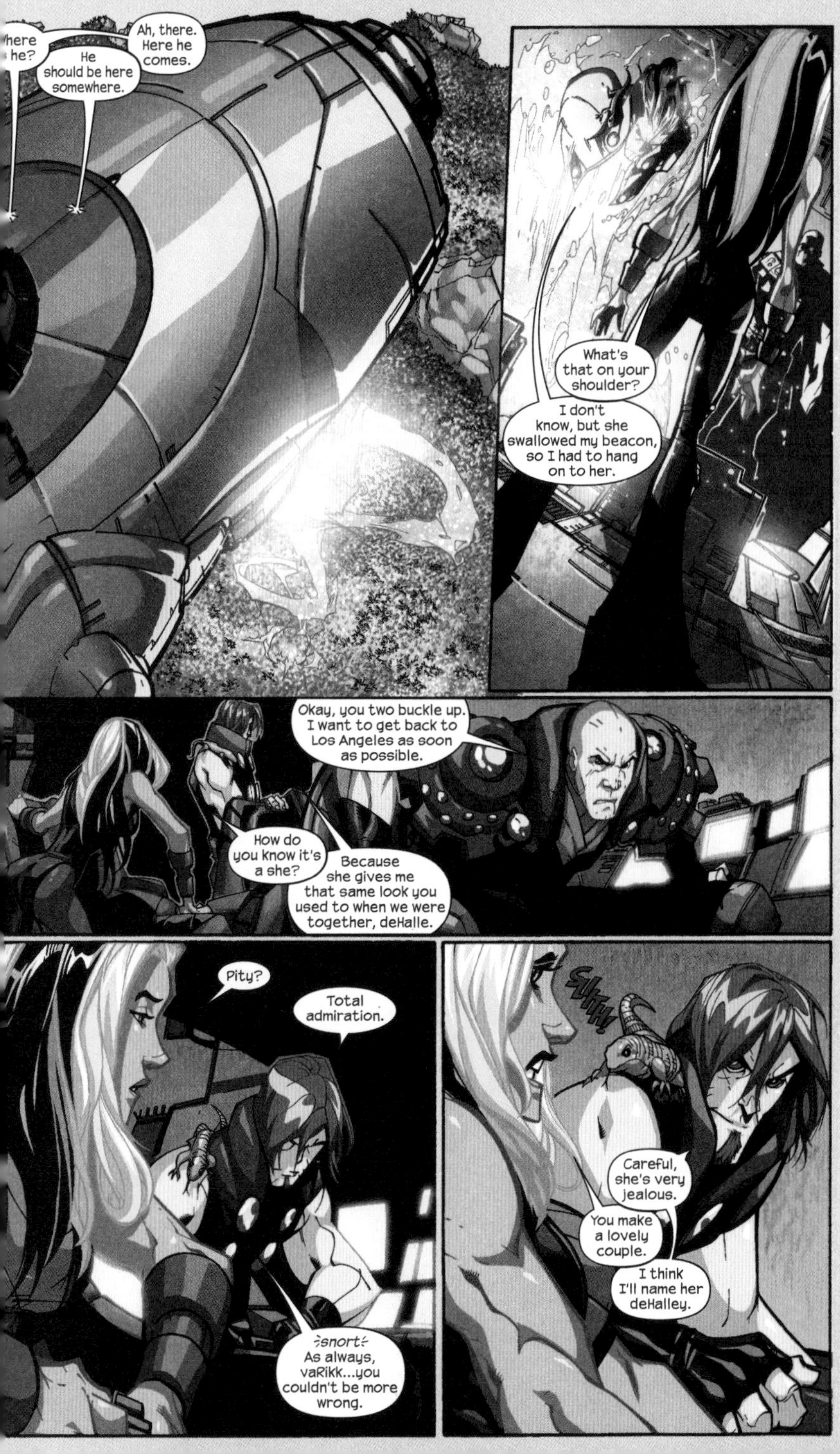

He should be here somewhere.
Ah, there. Here he comes.
What's that on your shoulder?
I don't know, but she swallowed my beacon, so I had to hang on to her.
Okay, you two buckle up. I want to get back to Los Angeles as soon as possible.
How do you know it's a she?
Because she gives me that same look you used to when we were together, deHalle.
Pity?
Total admiration.
<snort> As always, vaRikk...you couldn't be more wrong.
Careful, she's very jealous.
You make a lovely couple.
I think I'll name her deHalley.

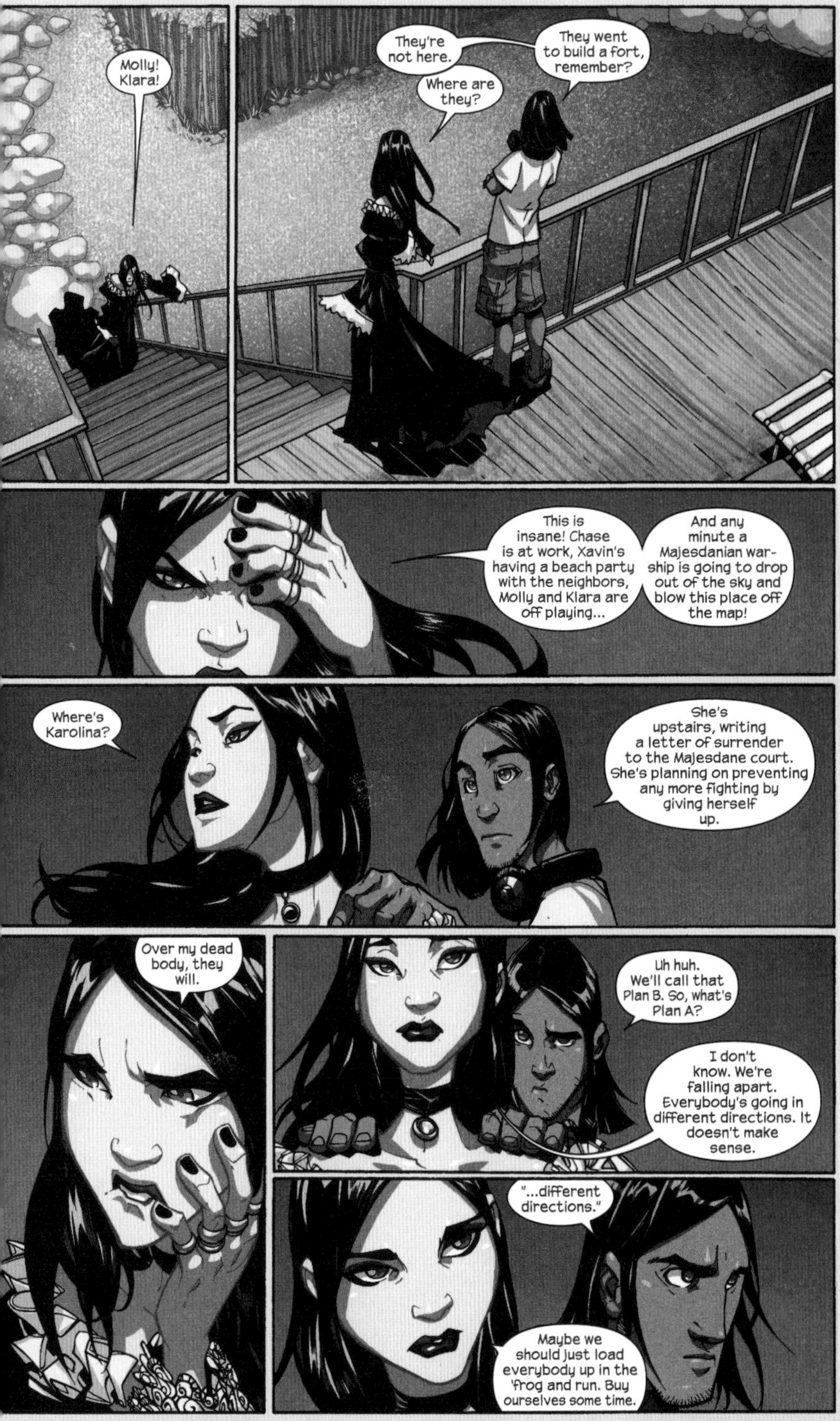
Molly! Klara!
They're not here.
Where are they?
They went to build a fort, remember?
This is insane! Chase is at work, Xavin's having a beach party with the neighbors, Molly and Klara are off playing...
And any minute a Majesdanian war-ship is going to drop out of the sky and blow this place off the map!
Where's Karolina?
She's upstairs, writing a letter of surrender to the Majesdane court. She's planning on preventing any more fighting by giving herself up.
Over my dead body, they will.
Uh huh. We'll call that Plan B. So, what's Plan A?
I don't know. We're falling apart. Everybody's going in different directions. It doesn't make sense.
"...different directions."
Maybe we should just load everybody up in the 'frog and run. Buy ourselves some time.

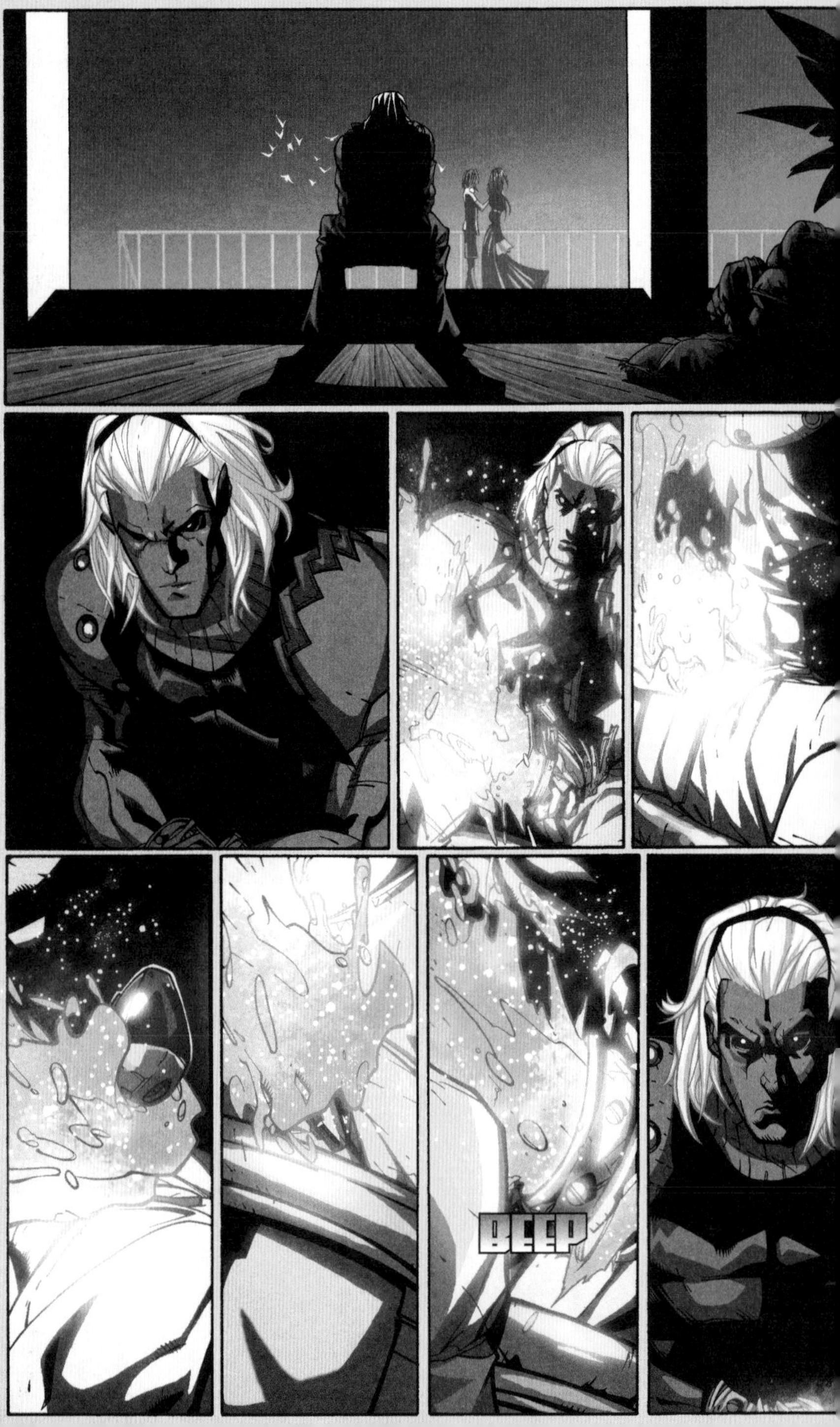
BEEP

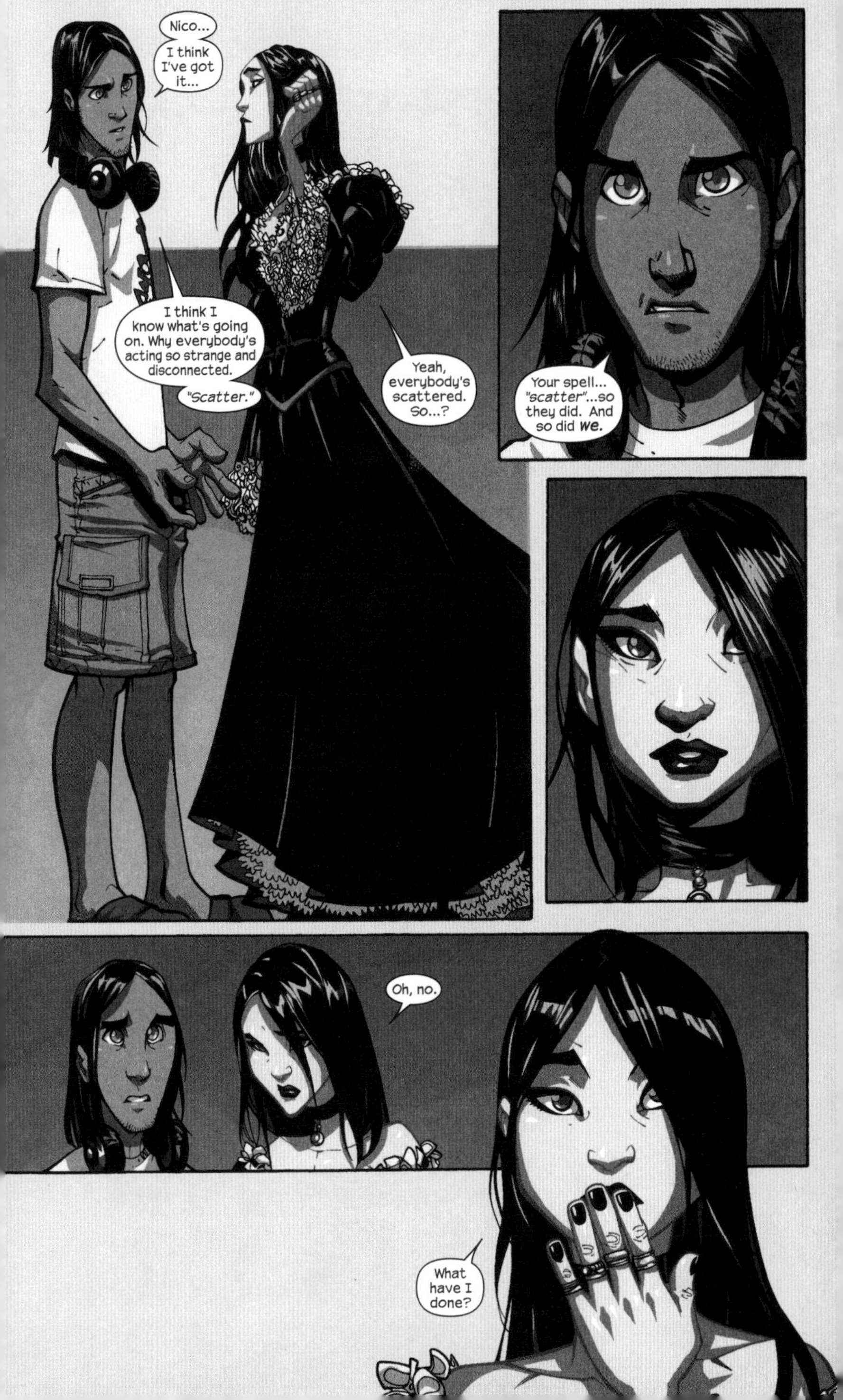
Nico...
I think I've got it...
I think I know what's going on. Why everybody's acting so strange and disconnected.
"Scatter."
Yeah, everybody's scattered. So...?
Your spell... "scatter"...so they did. And so did we.
Oh, no.
What have I done?

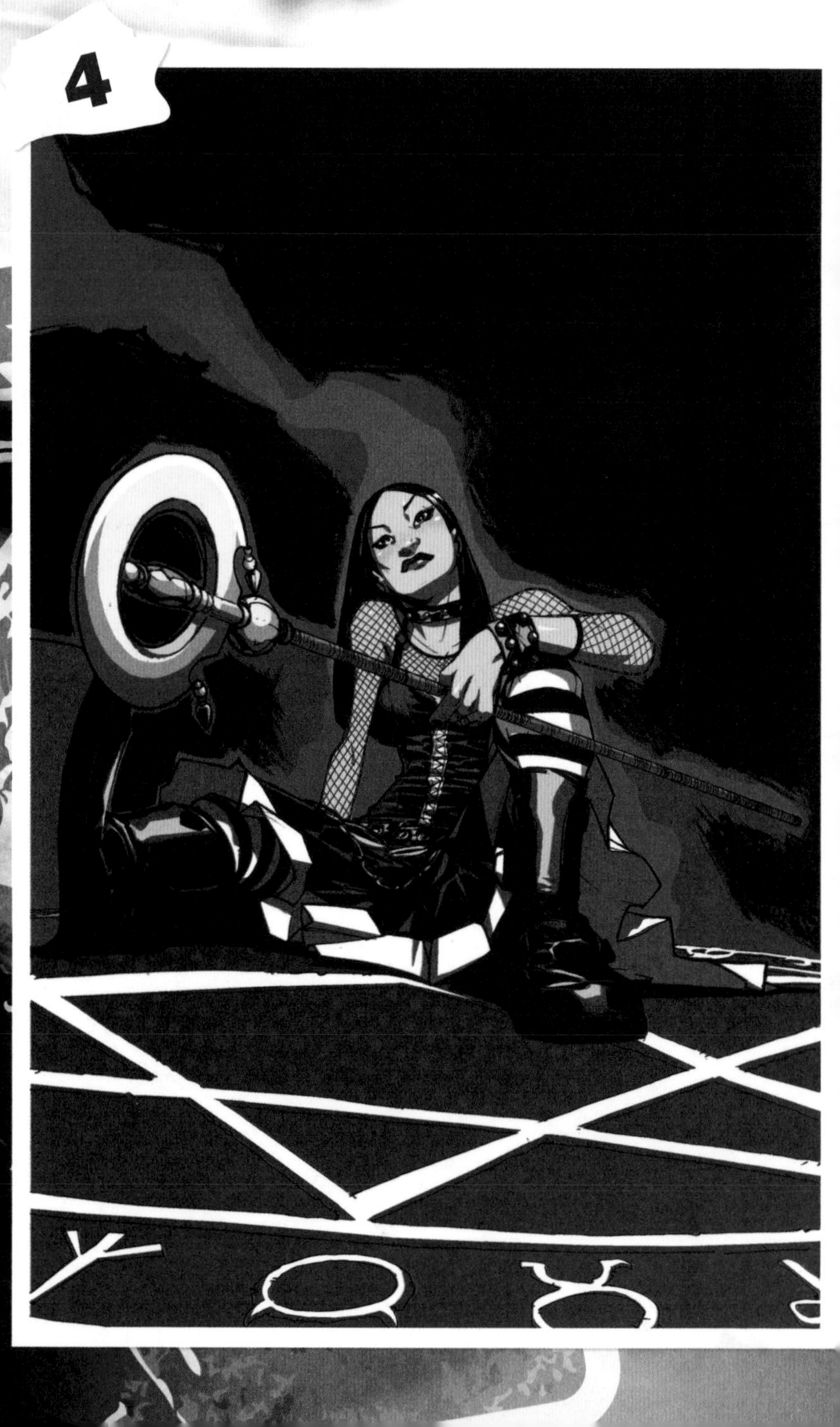
4

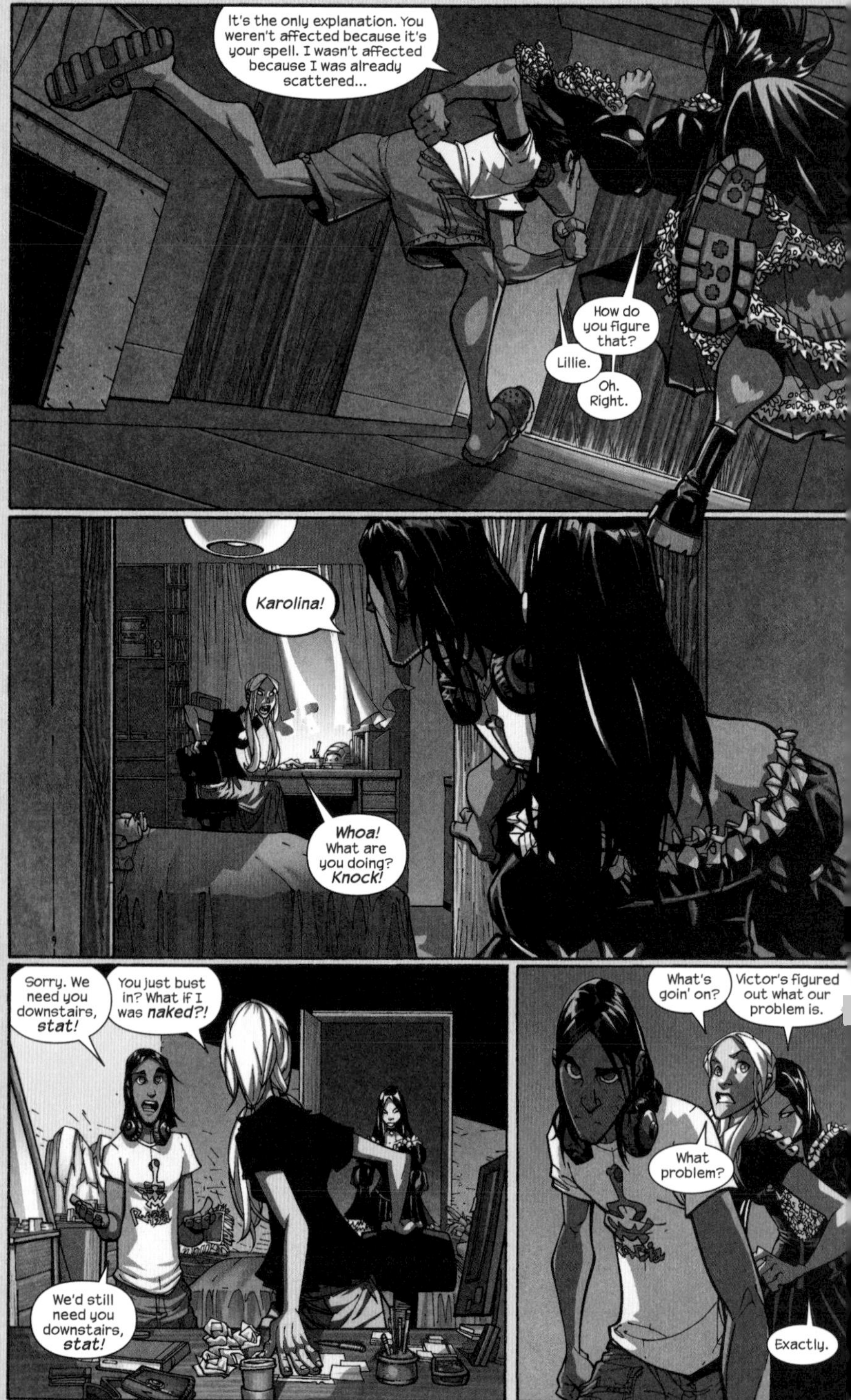
It's the only explanation. You weren't affected because it's your spell. I wasn't affected because I was already scattered...
How do you figure that?
Lillie.
Oh. Right.
Karolina!
Whoa! What are you doing? Knock!
Sorry. We need you downstairs, stat!
You just bust in? What if I was naked?!
We'd still need you downstairs, stat!
What's goin' on?
Victor's figured out what our problem is.
What problem?
Exactly.

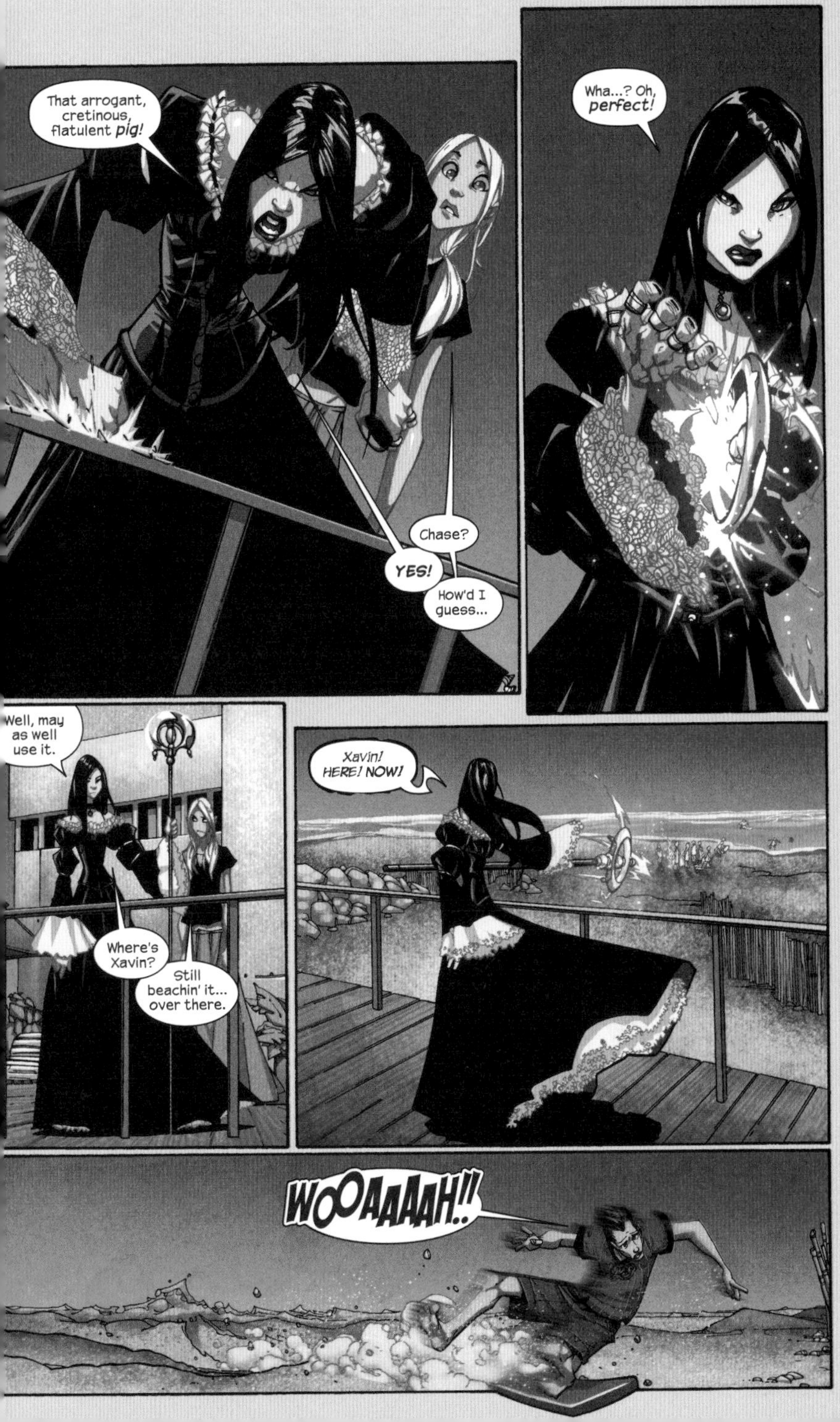

That arrogant, cretinous, flatulent *pig!*
Chase?
YES!
How'd I guess...
Wha...? Oh, *perfect!*
Well, may as well use it.
Where's Xavin?
Still beachin' it... over there.
Xavin! HERE! NOW!
WOOAAAAH!!

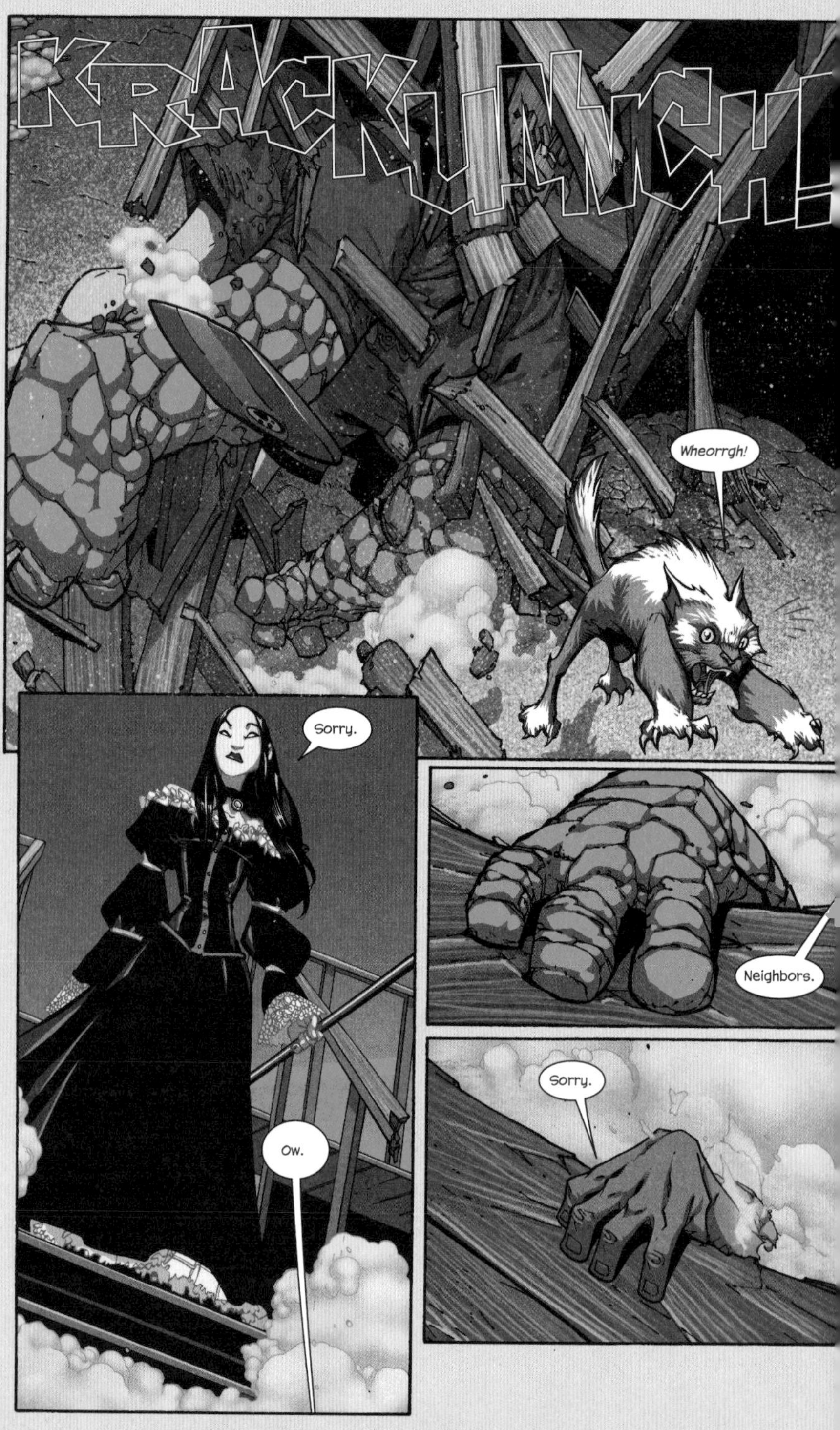
KRACKUNNCH!
Wheorrgh!
Sorry.
Ow.
Neighbors.
Sorry.

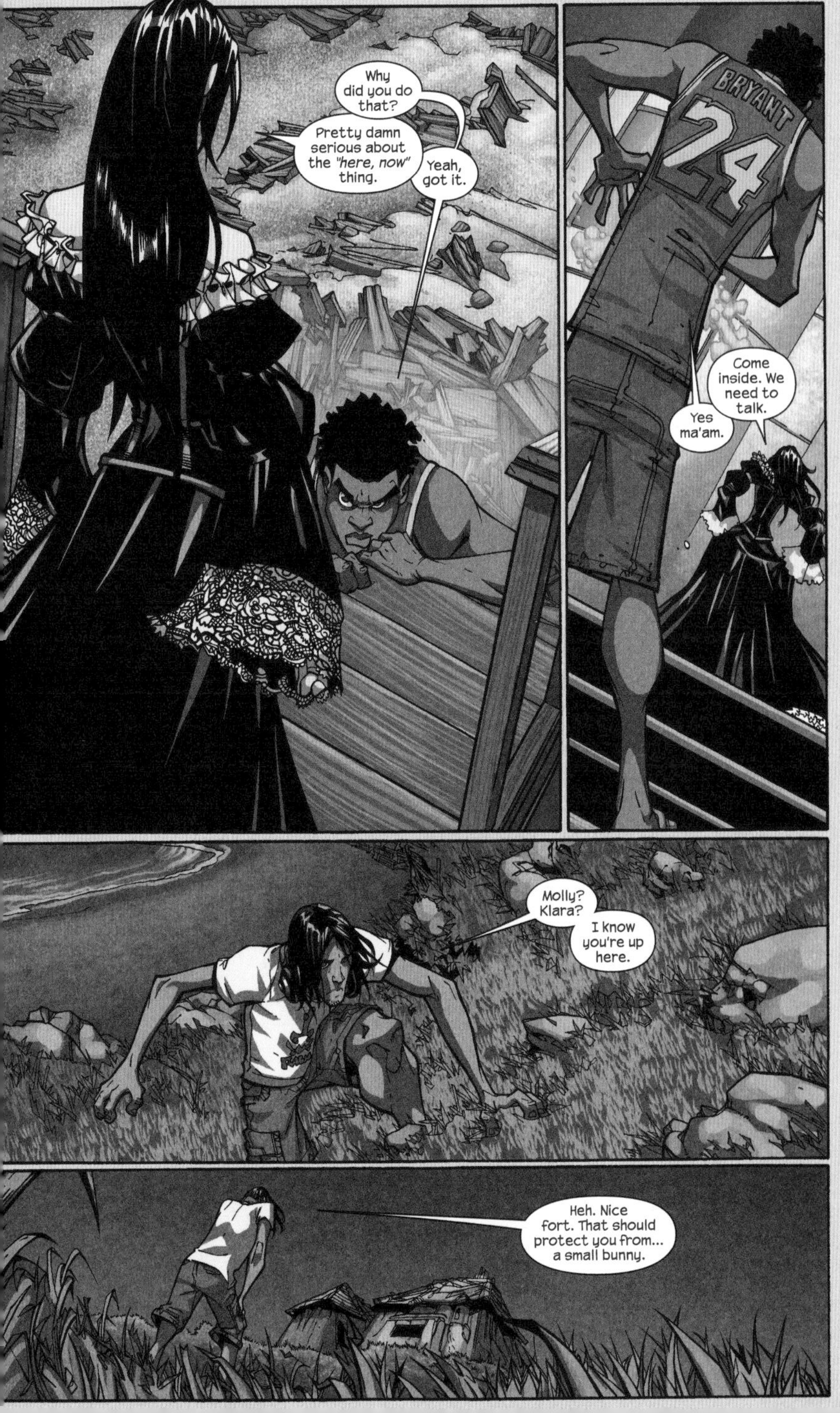
Why did you do that?
Pretty damn serious about the "here, now" thing.
Yeah, got it.
BRYANT 24
Come inside. We need to talk.
Yes ma'am.
Molly? Klara?
I know you're up here.
Heh. Nice fort. That should protect you from... a small bunny.

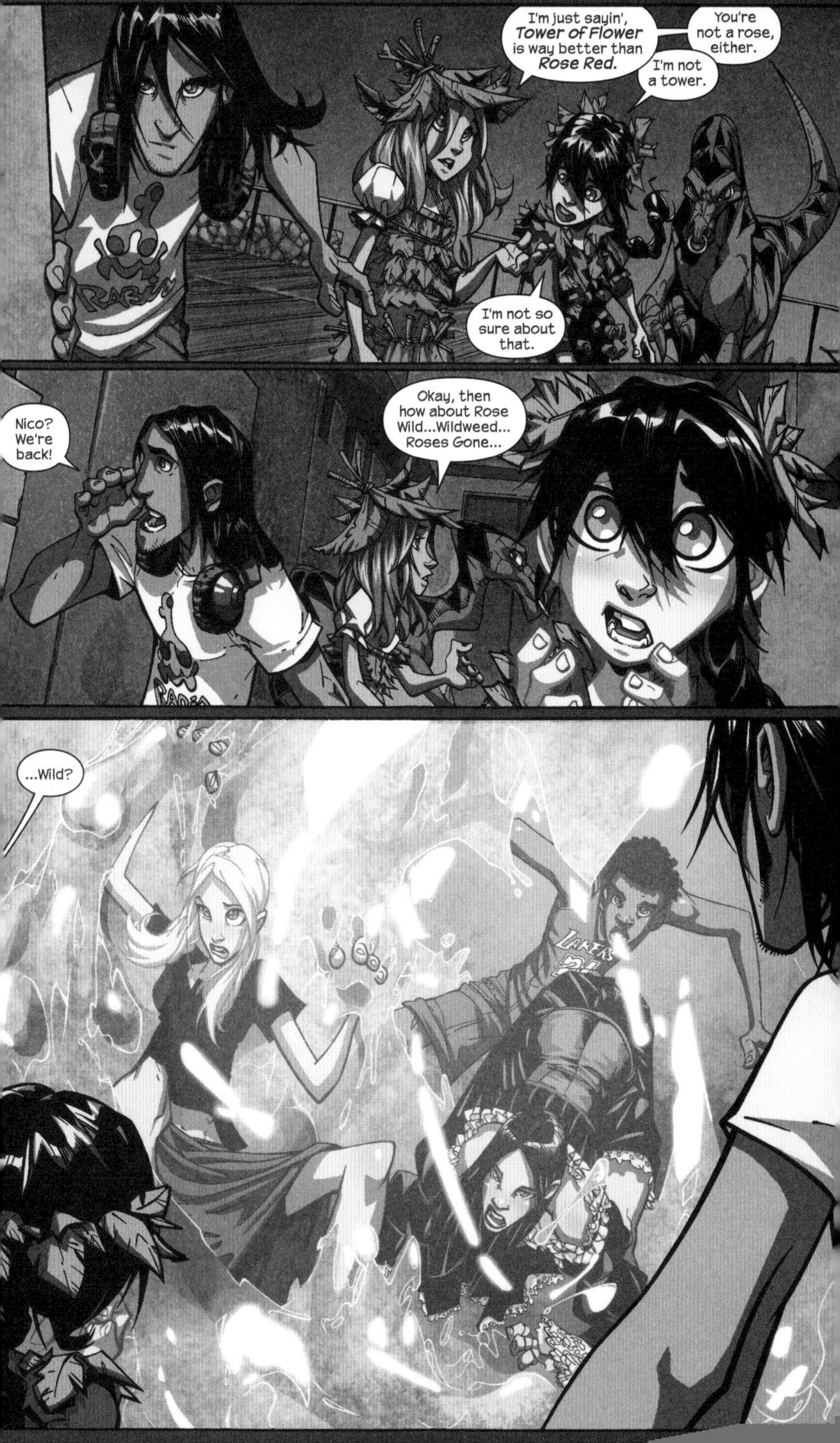
I'm just sayin', *Tower of Flower* is way better than *Rose Red.*
You're not a rose, either.
I'm not a tower.
I'm not so sure about that.
Nico? We're back!
Okay, then how about Rose Wild...Wildweed... Roses Gone...
...Wild?

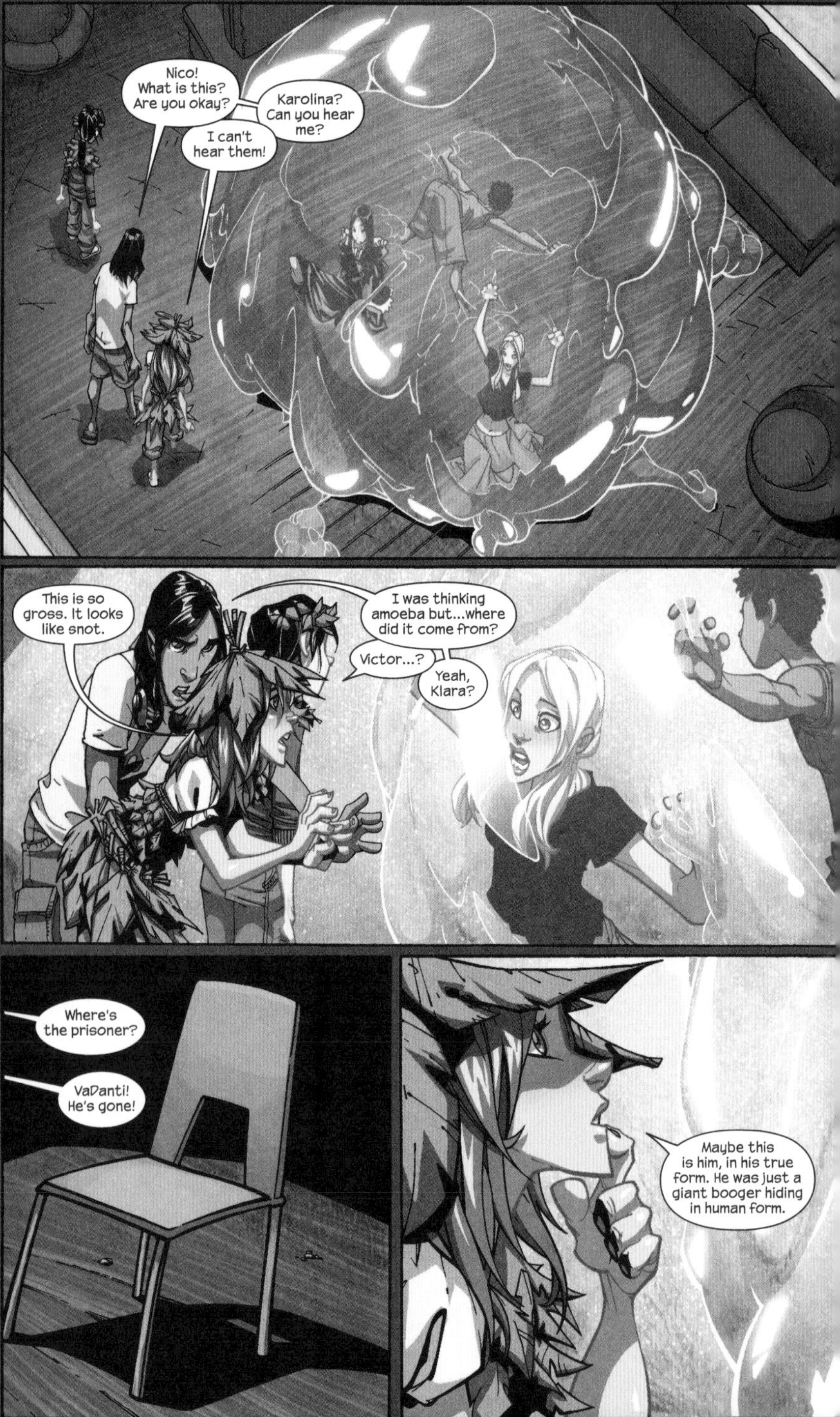

Nico! What is this? Are you okay?
Karolina? Can you hear me?
I can't hear them!
This is so gross. It looks like snot.
I was thinking amoeba but...where did it come from?
Victor...?
Yeah, Klara?
Where's the prisoner?
VaDanti! He's gone!
Maybe this is him, in his true form. He was just a giant booger hiding in human form.

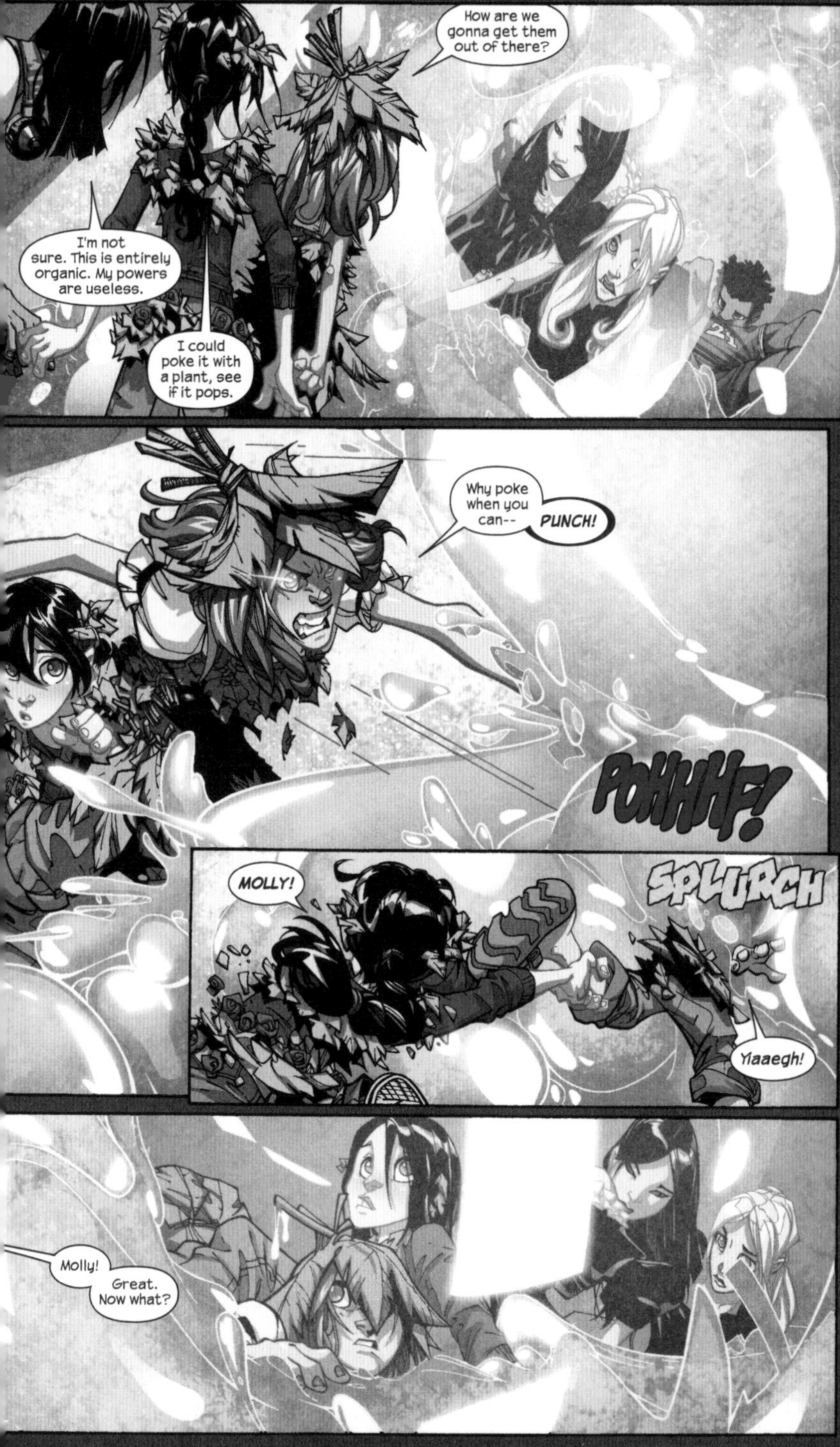

How are we gonna get them out of there?
I'm not sure. This is entirely organic. My powers are useless.
I could poke it with a plant, see if it pops.
Why poke when you can--
PUNCH!
POHHHF!
MOLLY!
SPLURCH
Yiaaegh!
Molly!
Great. Now what?

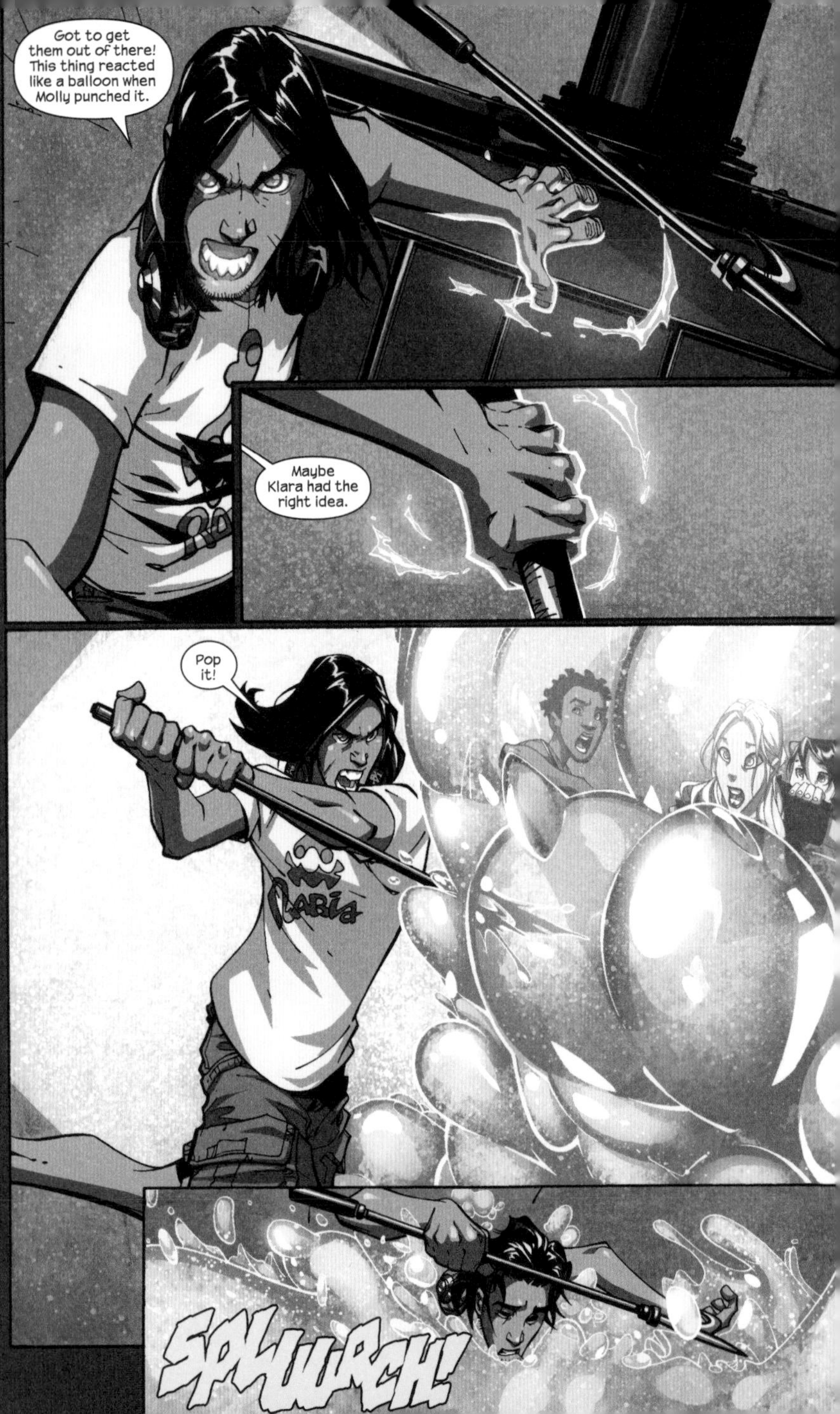
Got to get them out of there! This thing reacted like a balloon when Molly punched it.
Maybe Klara had the right idea.
Pop it!
SPLUURCH!

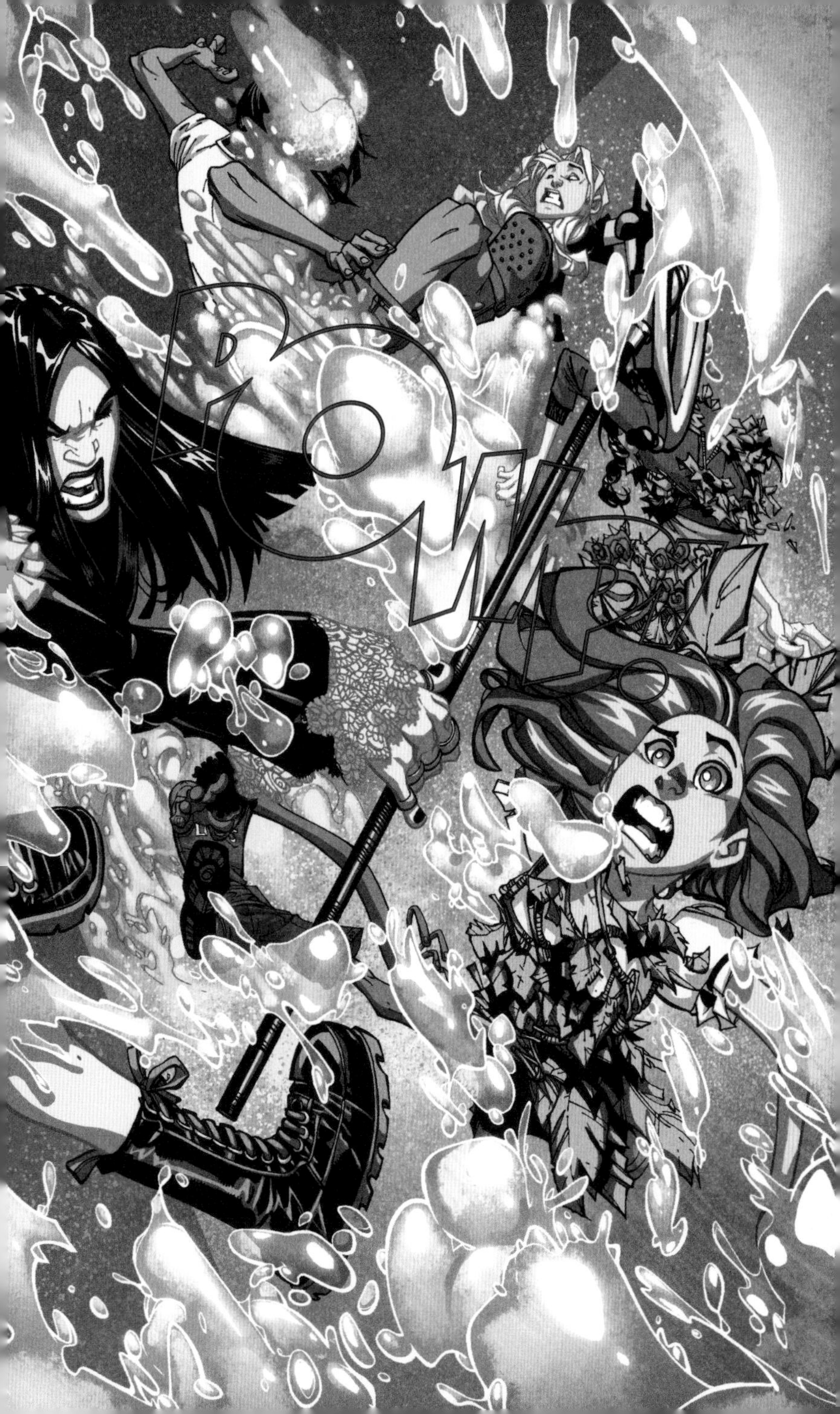
POW!

5

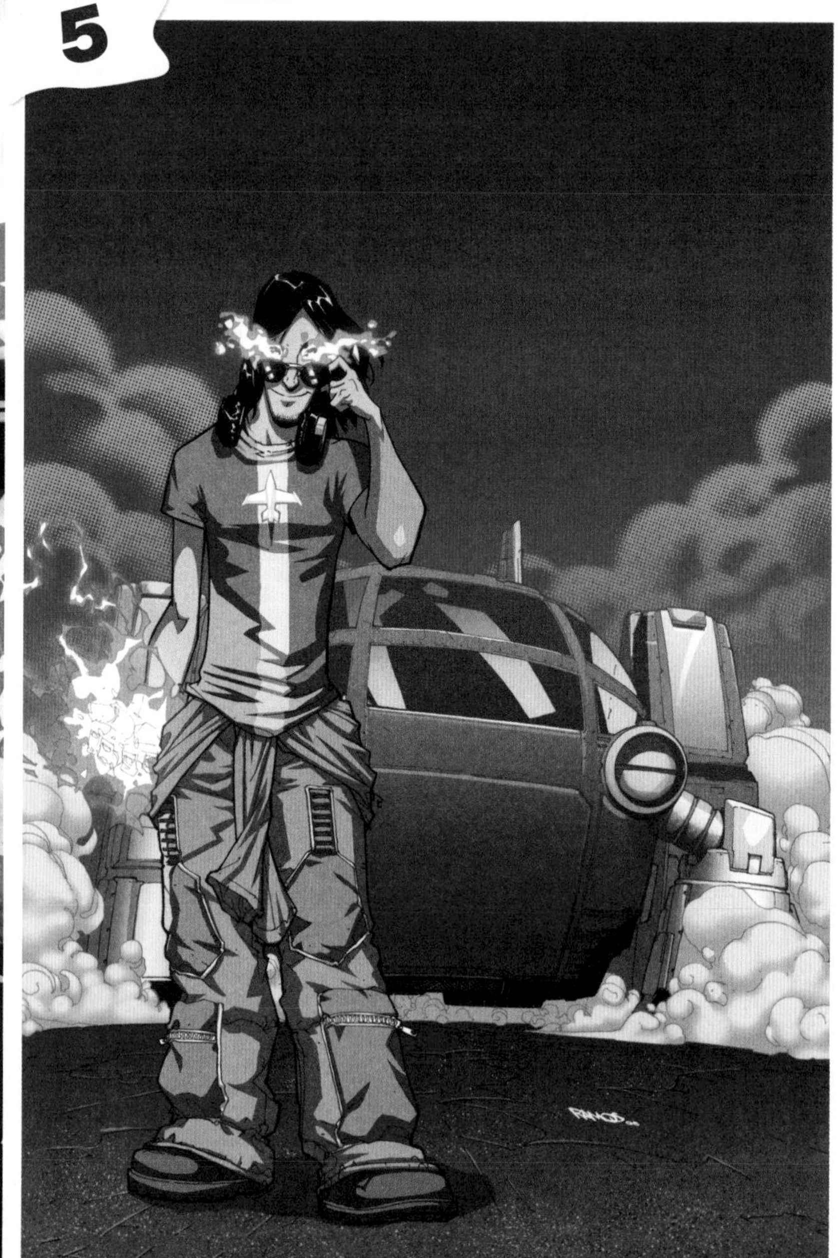

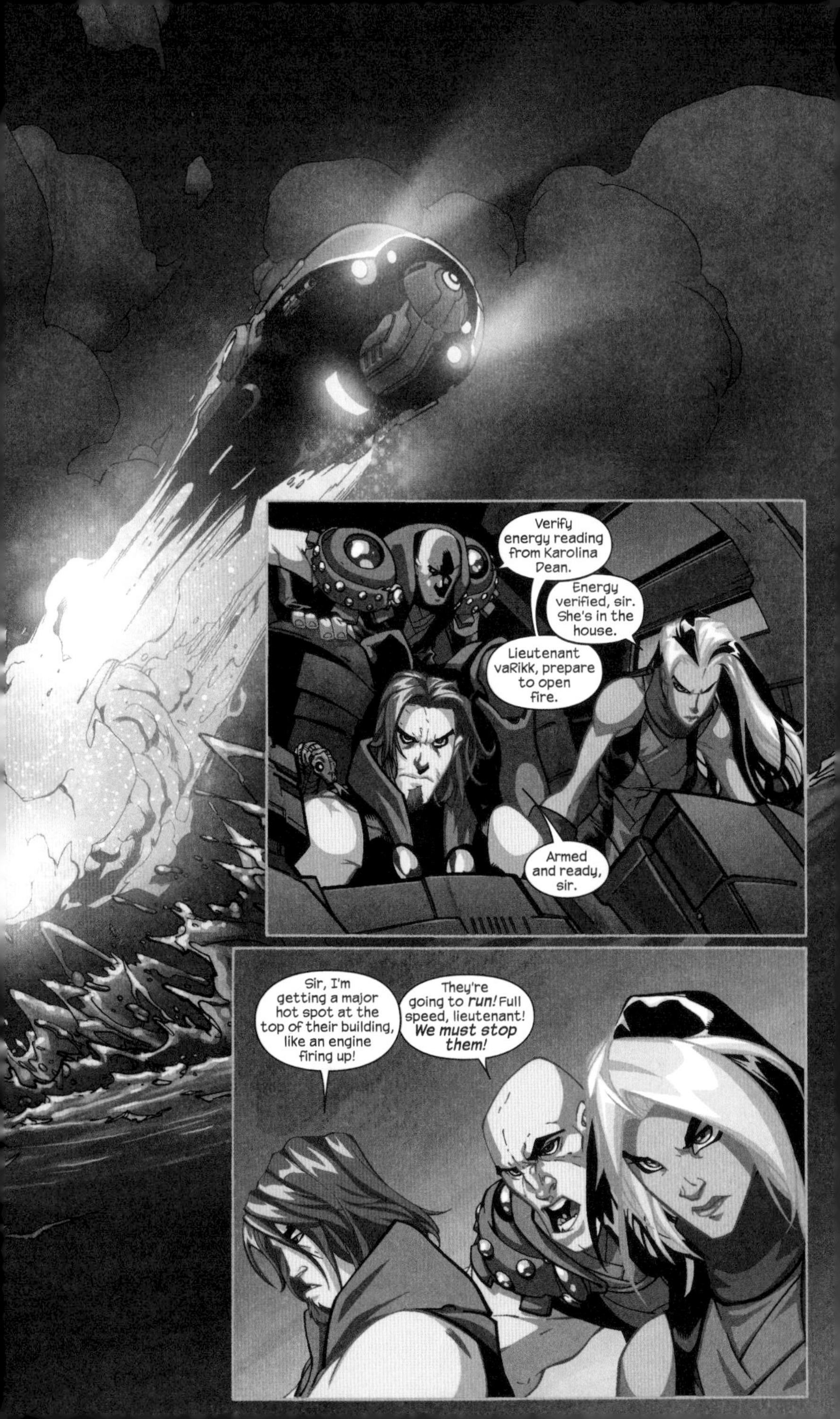
Verify energy reading from Karolina Dean.
Energy verified, sir. She's in the house.
Lieutenant vaRikk, prepare to open fire.
Armed and ready, sir.
Sir, I'm getting a major hot spot at the top of their building, like an engine firing up!
They're going to *run!* Full speed, lieutenant! ***We must stop them!***

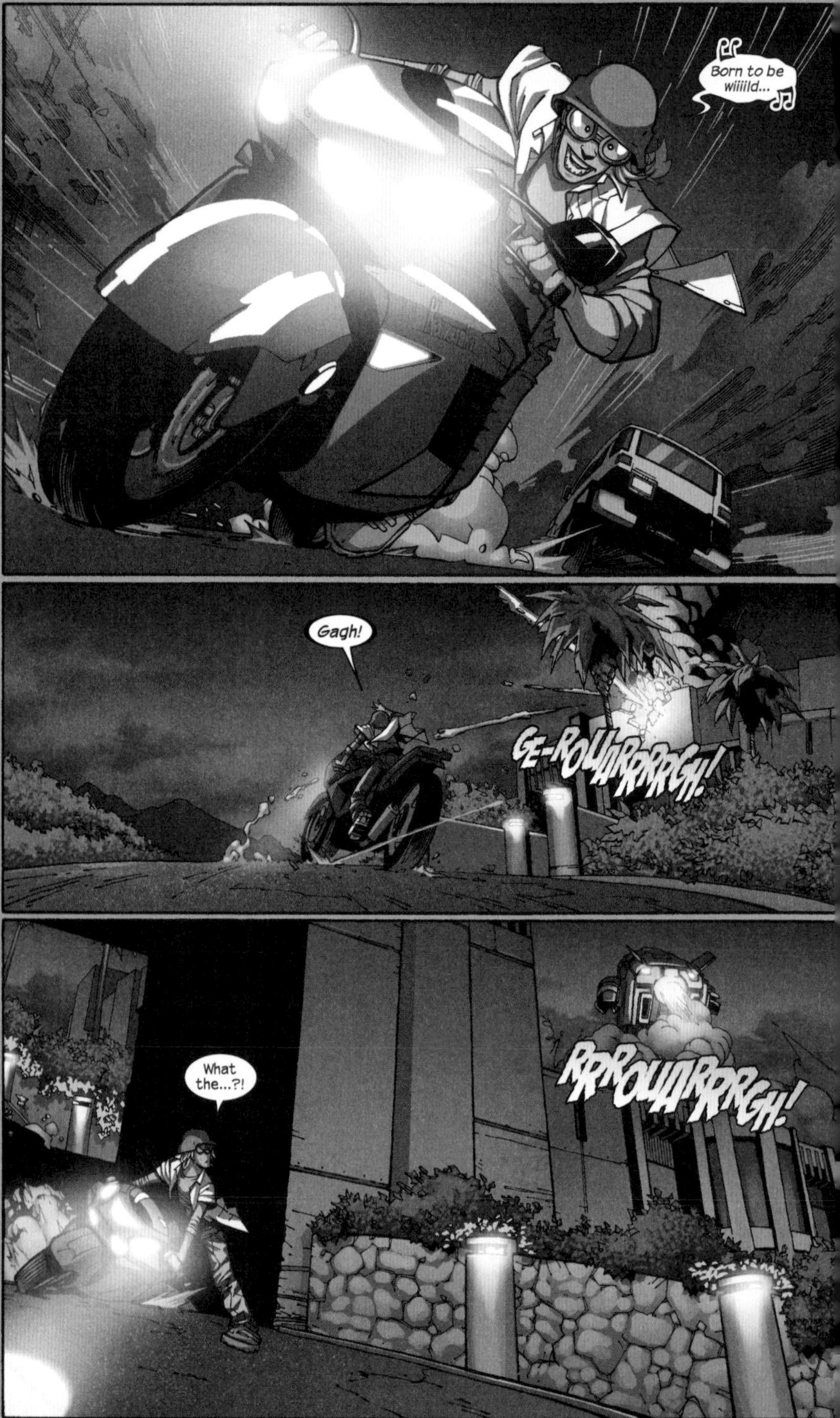
Born to be wiiiild...
Gagh!
GE-ROWARRRRGH!
What the...?!
RRROWARRRGH!

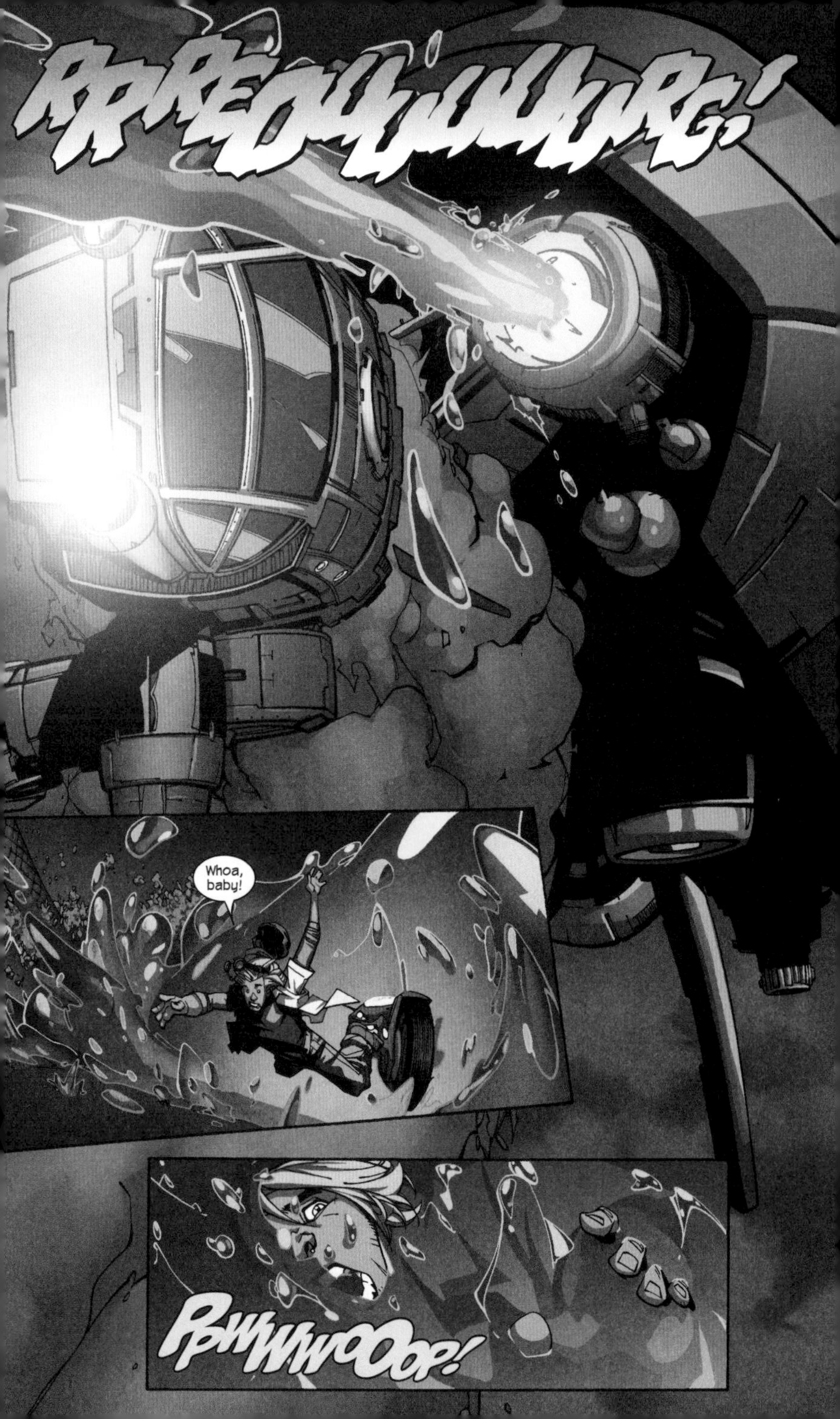
RRRREOWWWWRG!
Whoa, baby!
PSHWWWOOOP!

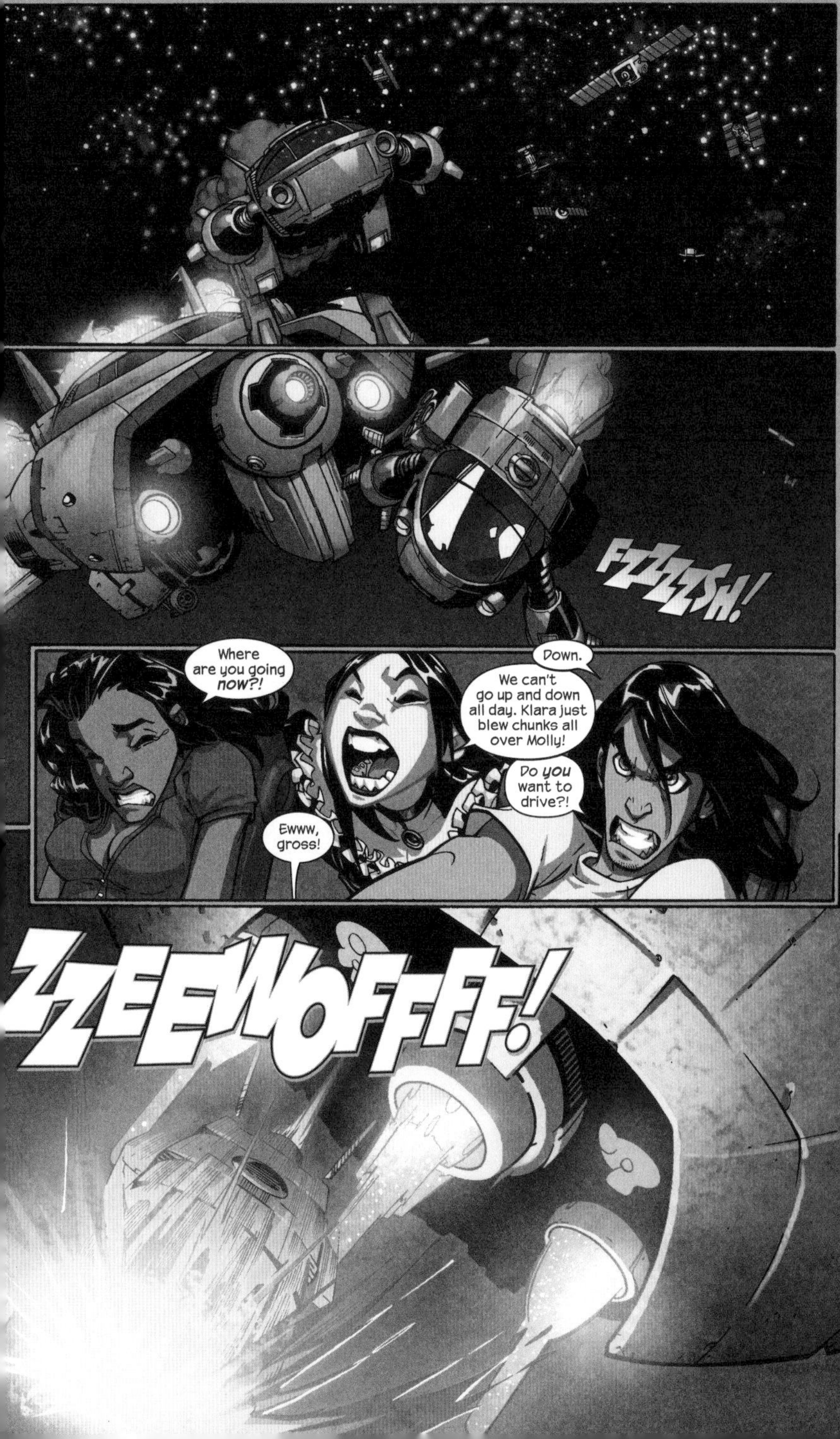
FZZZZSH!
Where are you going *now*?!
Down.
We can't go up and down all day. Klara just blew chunks all over Molly!
Do *you* want to drive?!
Ewww, gross!
ZZEEWOFFFF!

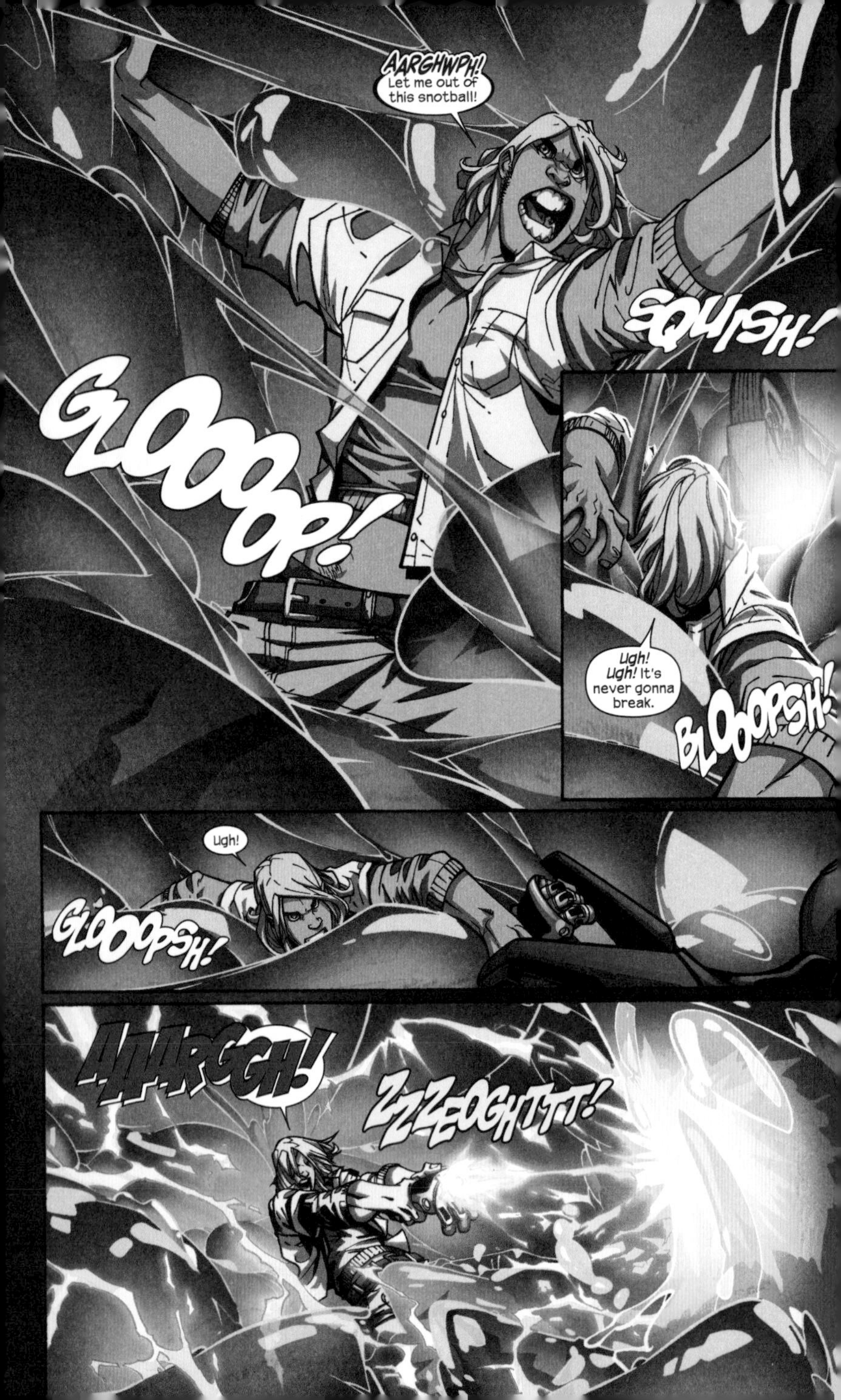
AARGHWPH!
Let me out of this snotball!
SQUISH!
GLOOOOOP!
Ugh! Ugh! It's never gonna break.
BLOOOPSH!
Ugh!
GLOOOPSH!
AAARGGH!
ZZZEOGHTTTT!

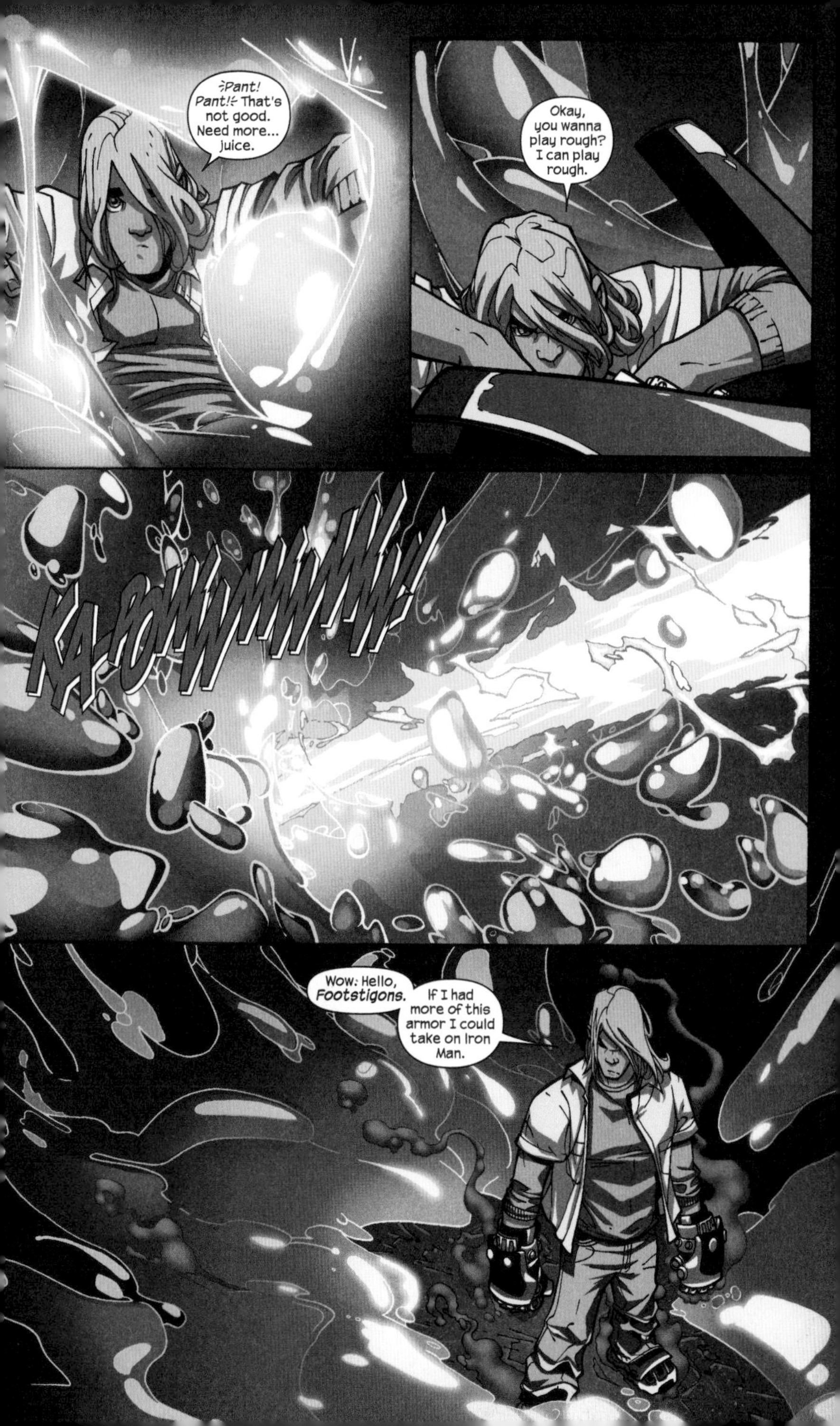

Pant! Pant! That's not good. Need more... juice.
Okay, you wanna play rough? I can play rough.
KA-POWWWWWWW!
Wow: Hello, Footstigons.
If I had more of this armor I could take on Iron Man.

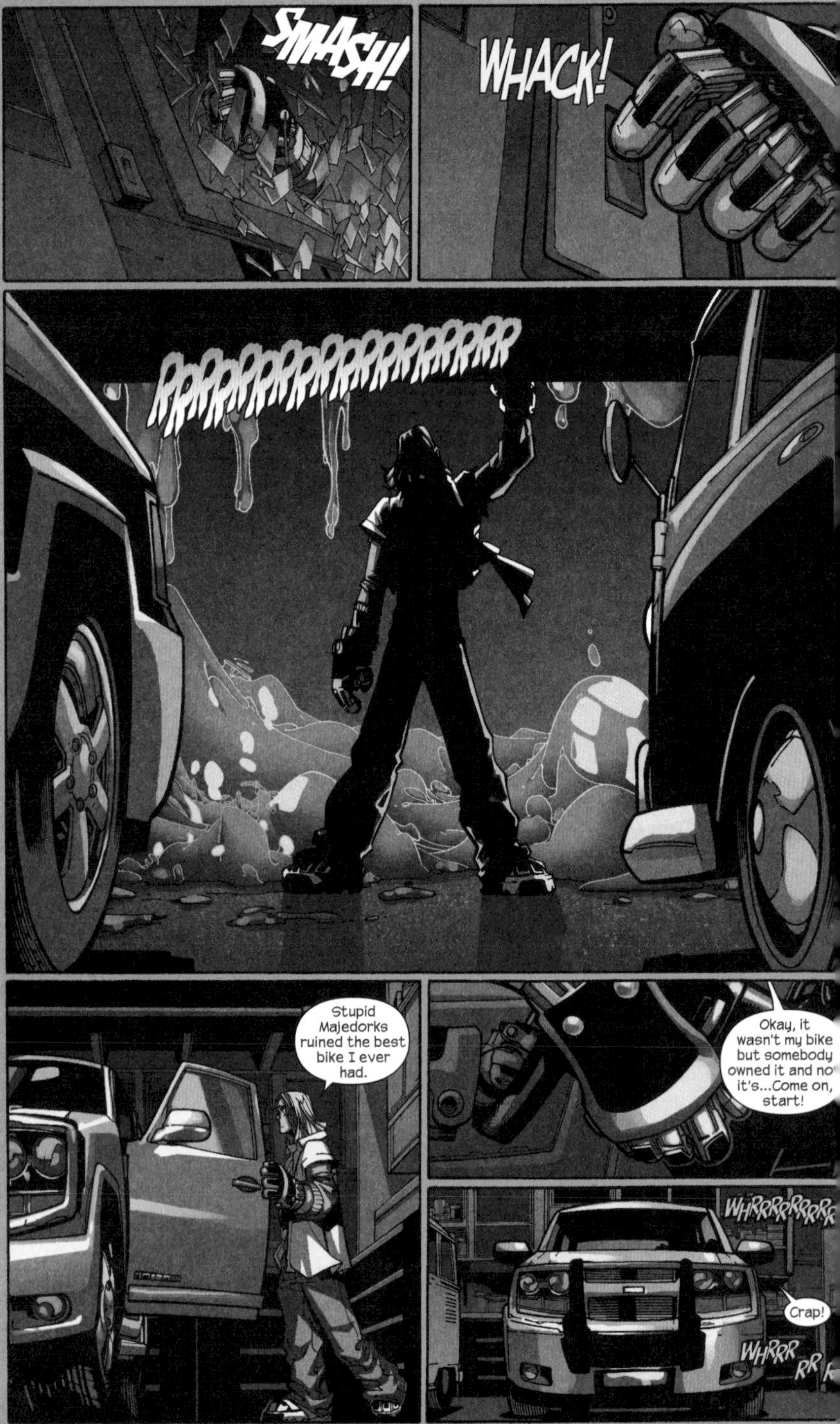
SMASH!
WHACK!
RRRRRRRRRRRRRRRRRRRRRRRRRR
Stupid Majedorks ruined the best bike I ever had.
Okay, it wasn't my bike but somebody owned it and no it's...Come on, start!
WHRRRRRRRRR
Crap!
WHRRR RR R

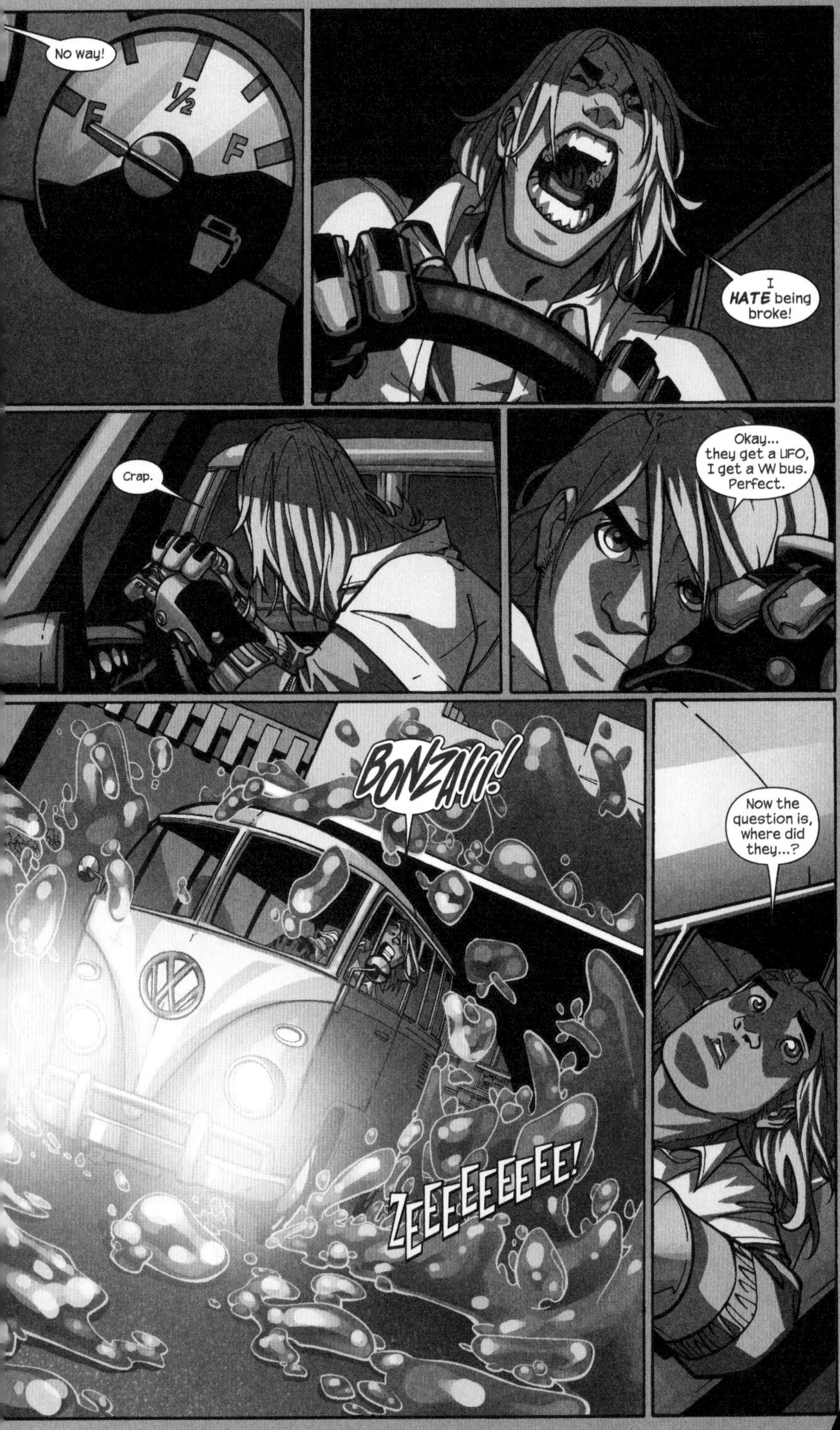
No way!
I HATE being broke!
Crap.
Okay... they get a UFO, I get a VW bus. Perfect.
BONZAI!!!
ZEEEEEEEEE!
Now the question is, where did they...?

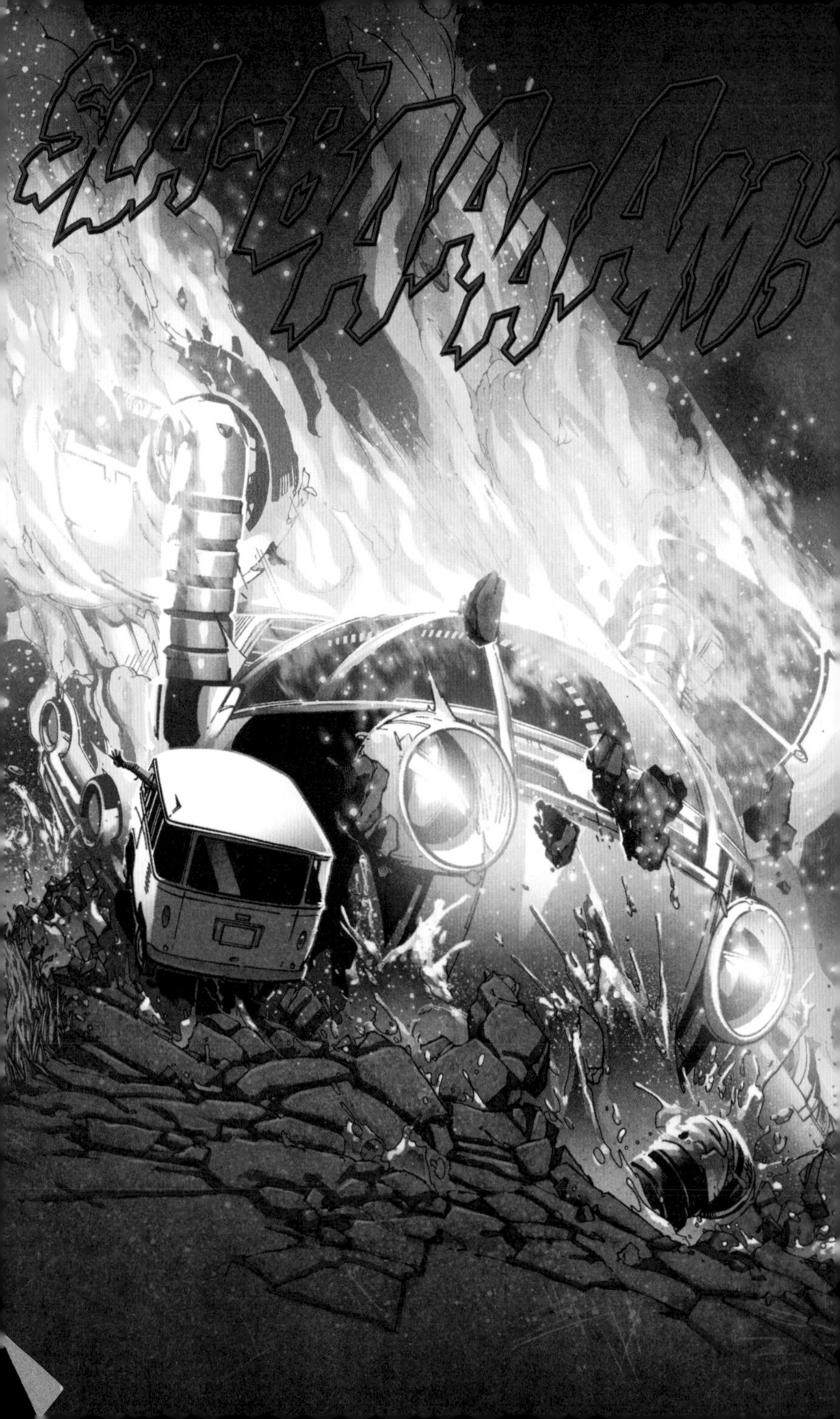

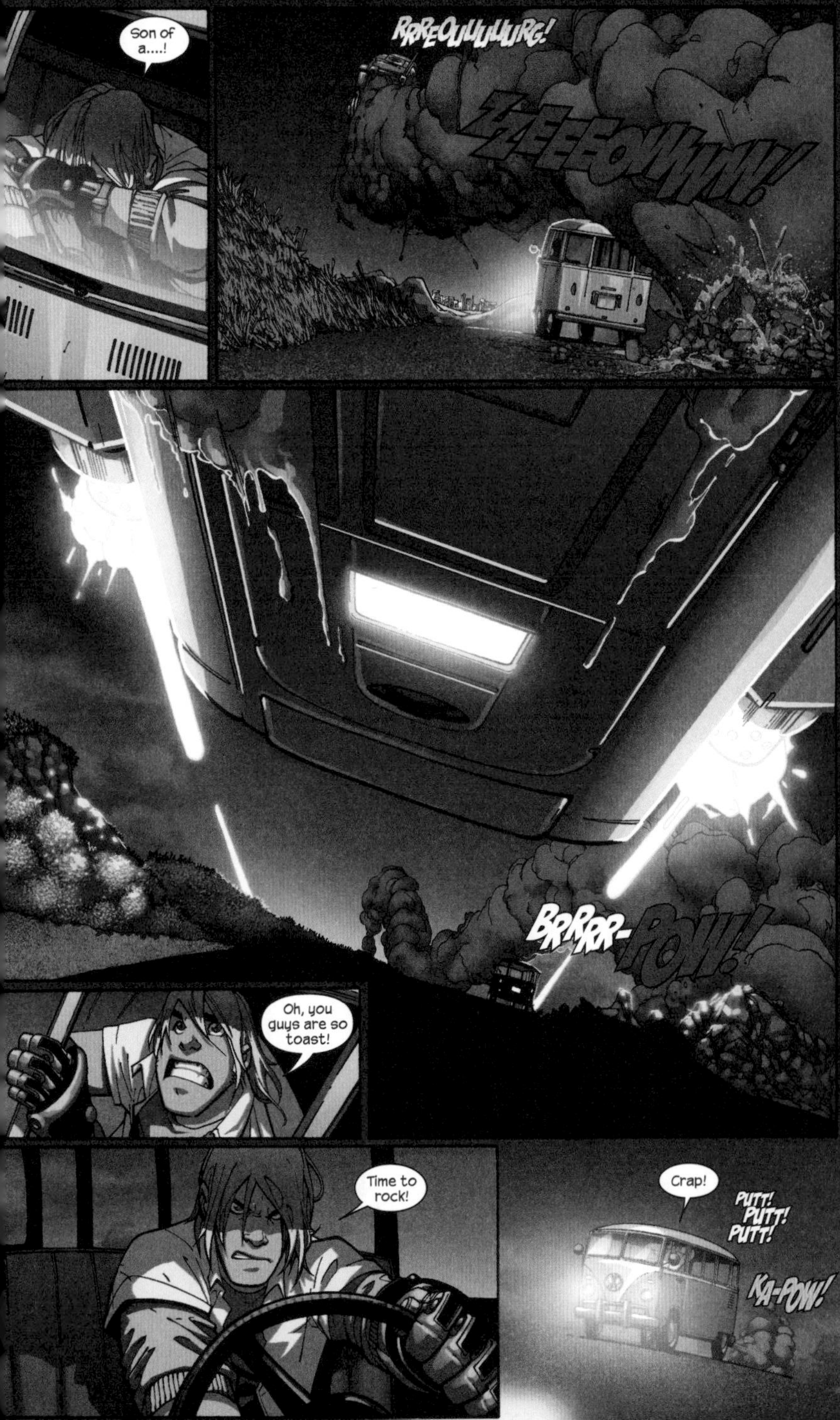
Son of a....!
RRRREOUUUUURG!
ZZEEEOWWW!
BRRRR-POW!
Oh, you guys are so toast!
Time to rock!
Crap!
PUTT! PUTT! PUTT!
KA-POW!

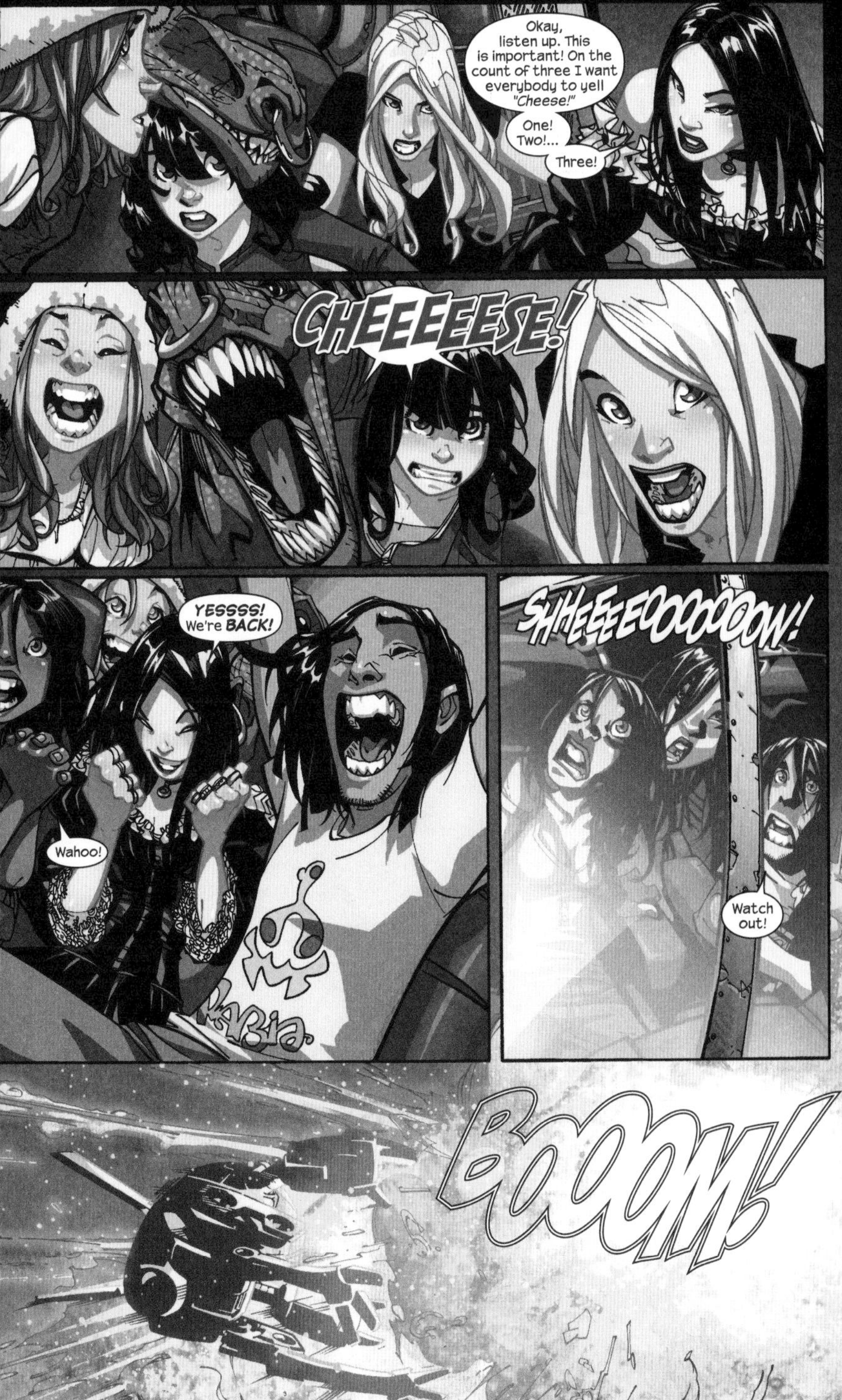

Okay, listen up. This is important! On the count of three I want everybody to yell "Cheese!"
One! Two!...
Three!
CHEEEEESE!
YESSSS! We're BACK!
Wahoo!
SHHEEEEOOOOOOW!
Watch out!
BOOOM!

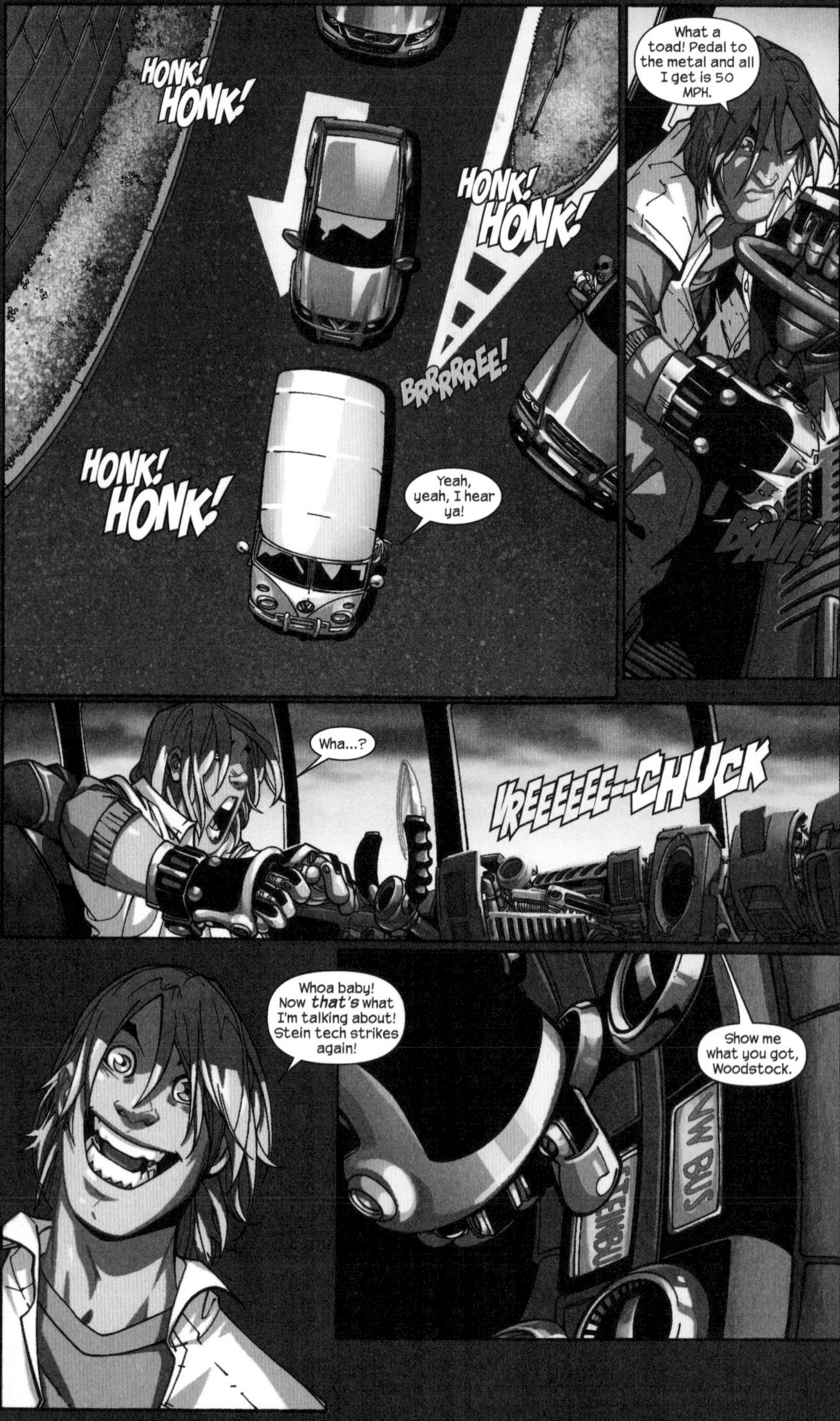
HONK! HONK!
HONK! HONK!
BRRRRRREE!
HONK! HONK!
Yeah, yeah, I hear ya!
What a toad! Pedal to the metal and all I get is 50 MPH.
Wha...?
VREEEEEE-CHUCK
Whoa baby! Now *that's* what I'm talking about! Stein tech strikes again!
Show me what you got, Woodstock.
VW BUS

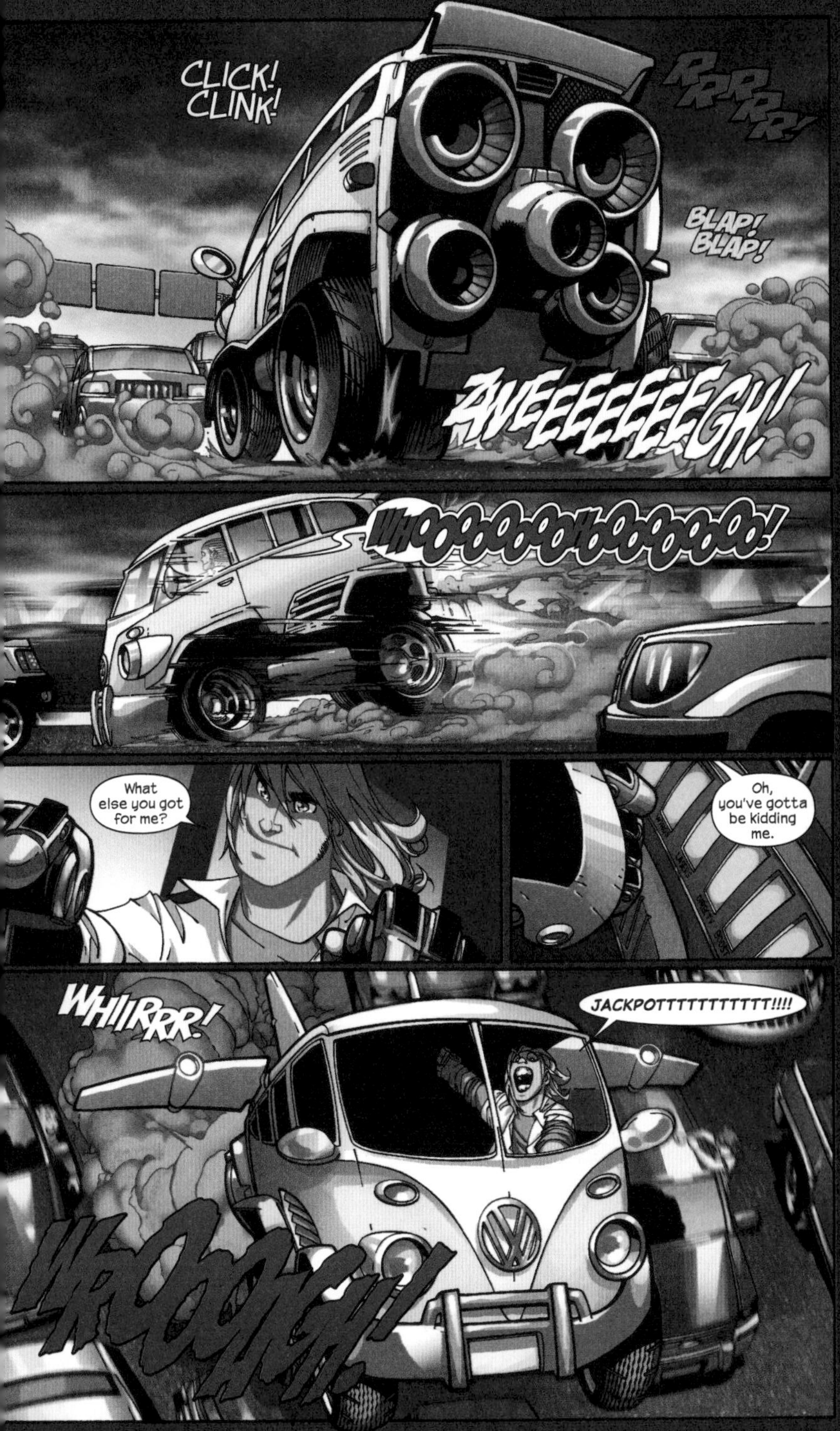

CLICK!
CLINK!
RRRRRR!
BLAP!
BLAP!
ZWEEEEEEEEGH!
WHOOOOOOOHOOOOOOO!
What else you got for me?
Oh, you've gotta be kidding me.
WHIIRRR!
JACKPOTTTTTTTTTTT!!!!
VROOOMGH!

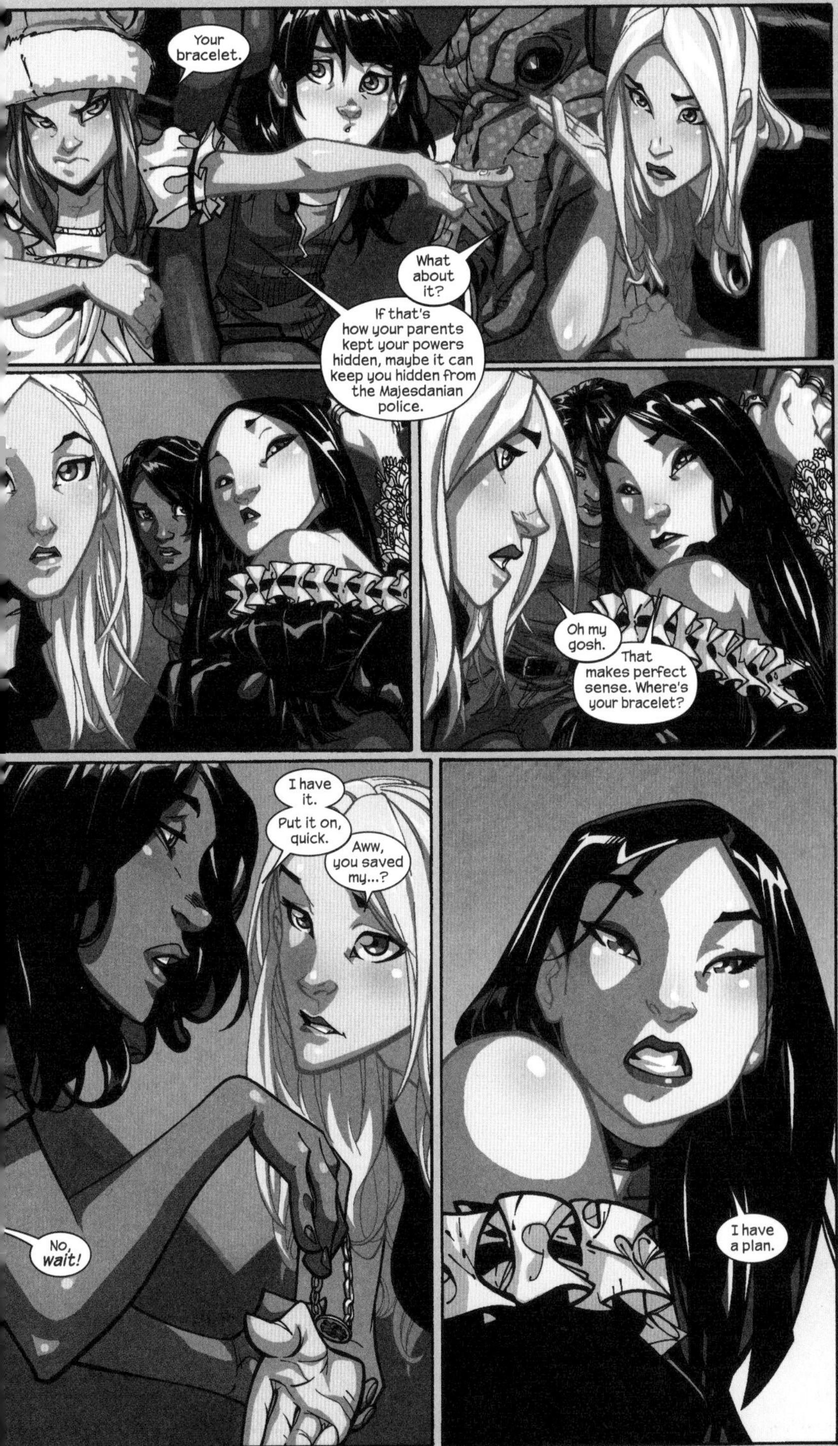
Your bracelet.
What about it?
If that's how your parents kept your powers hidden, maybe it can keep you hidden from the Majesdanian police.
Oh my gosh.
That makes perfect sense. Where's your bracelet?
I have it.
Put it on, quick.
Aww, you saved my...?
No, wait!
I have a plan.

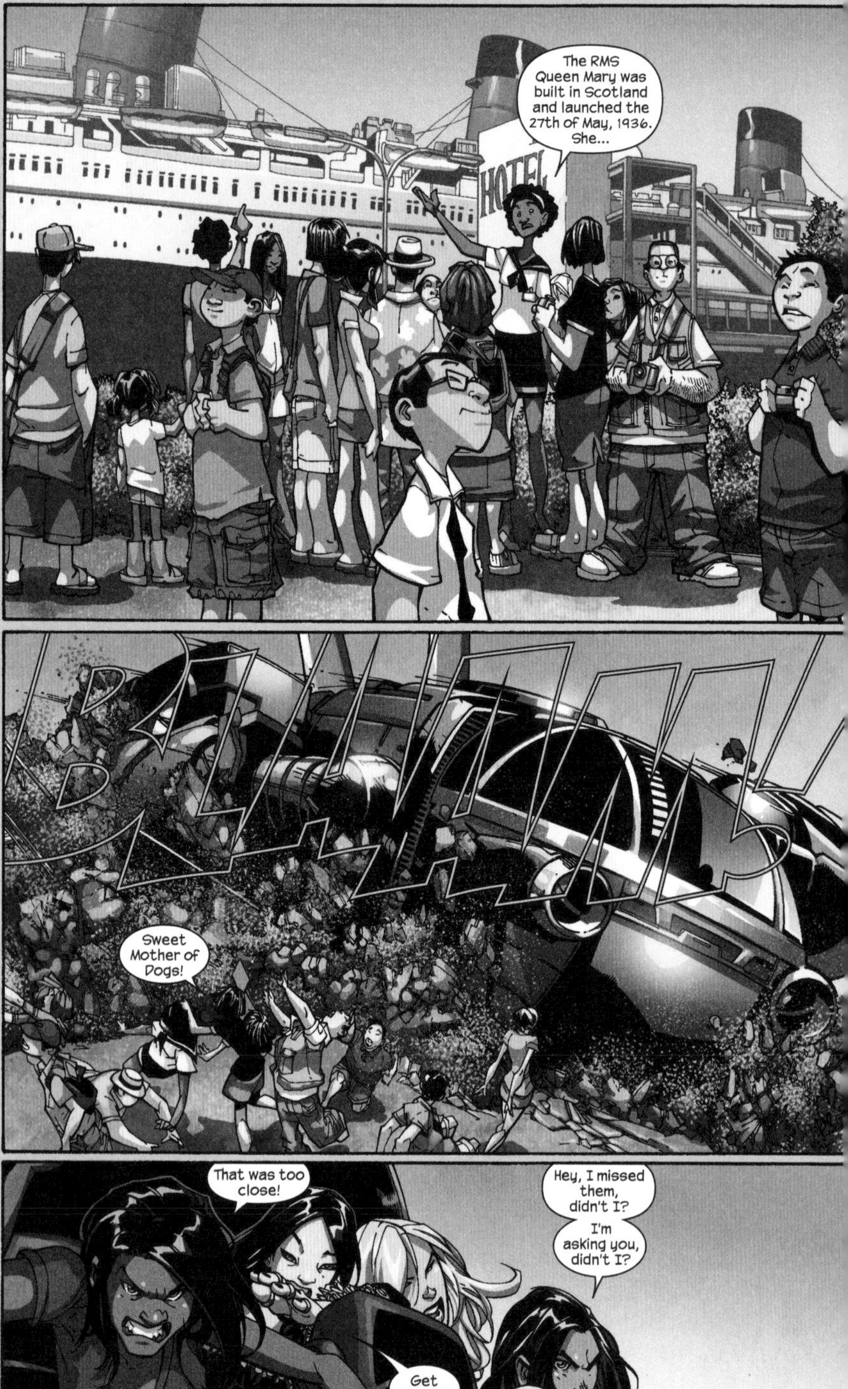

The RMS Queen Mary was built in Scotland and launched the 27th of May, 1936. She...
HOTEL
Sweet Mother of Dogs!
That was too close!
Hey, I missed them, didn't I?
I'm asking you, didn't I?
Get ready!

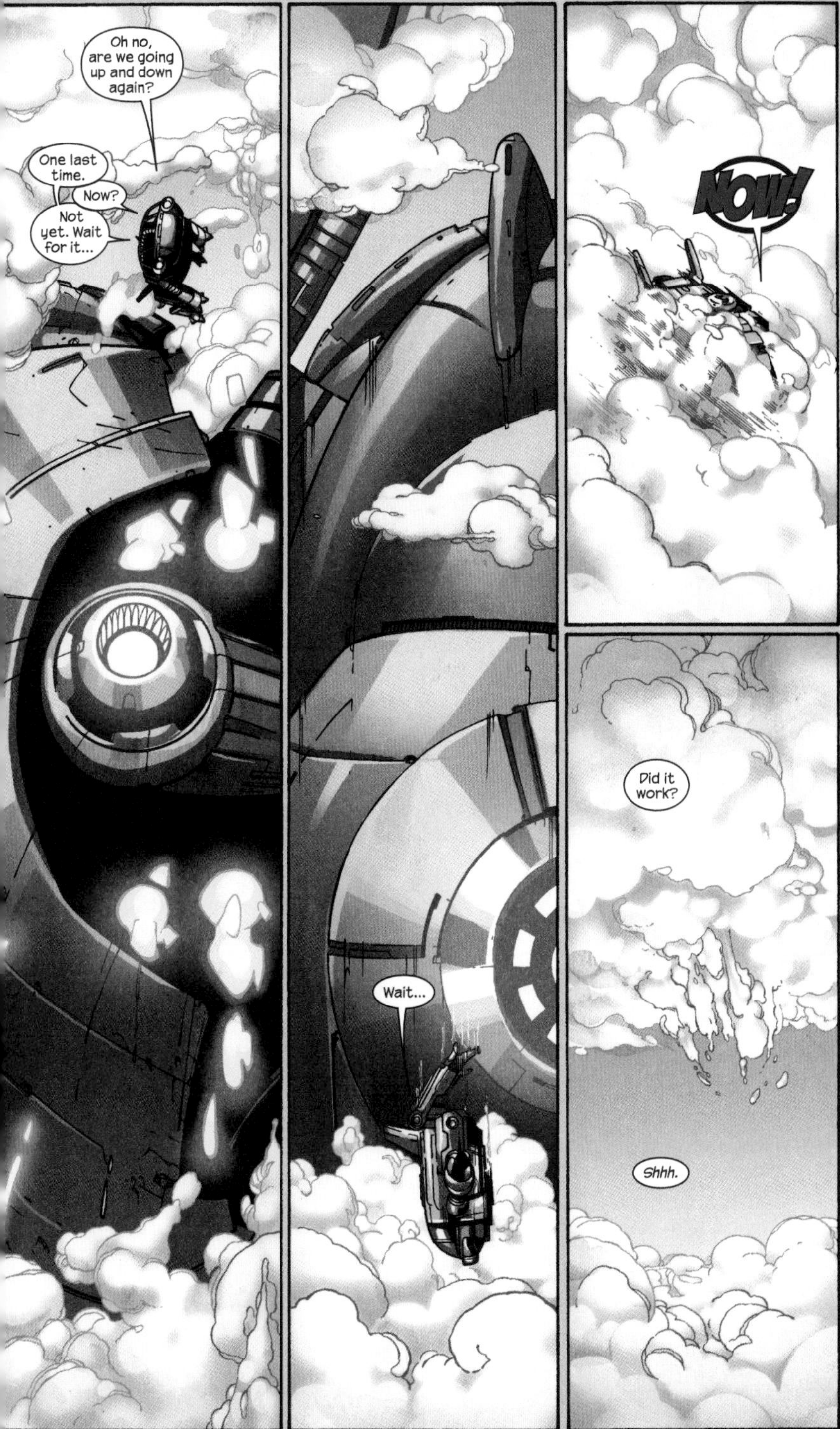
Oh no, are we going up and down again?
One last time.
Now?
Not yet. Wait for it...
Wait...
NOW!
Did it work?
Shhh.

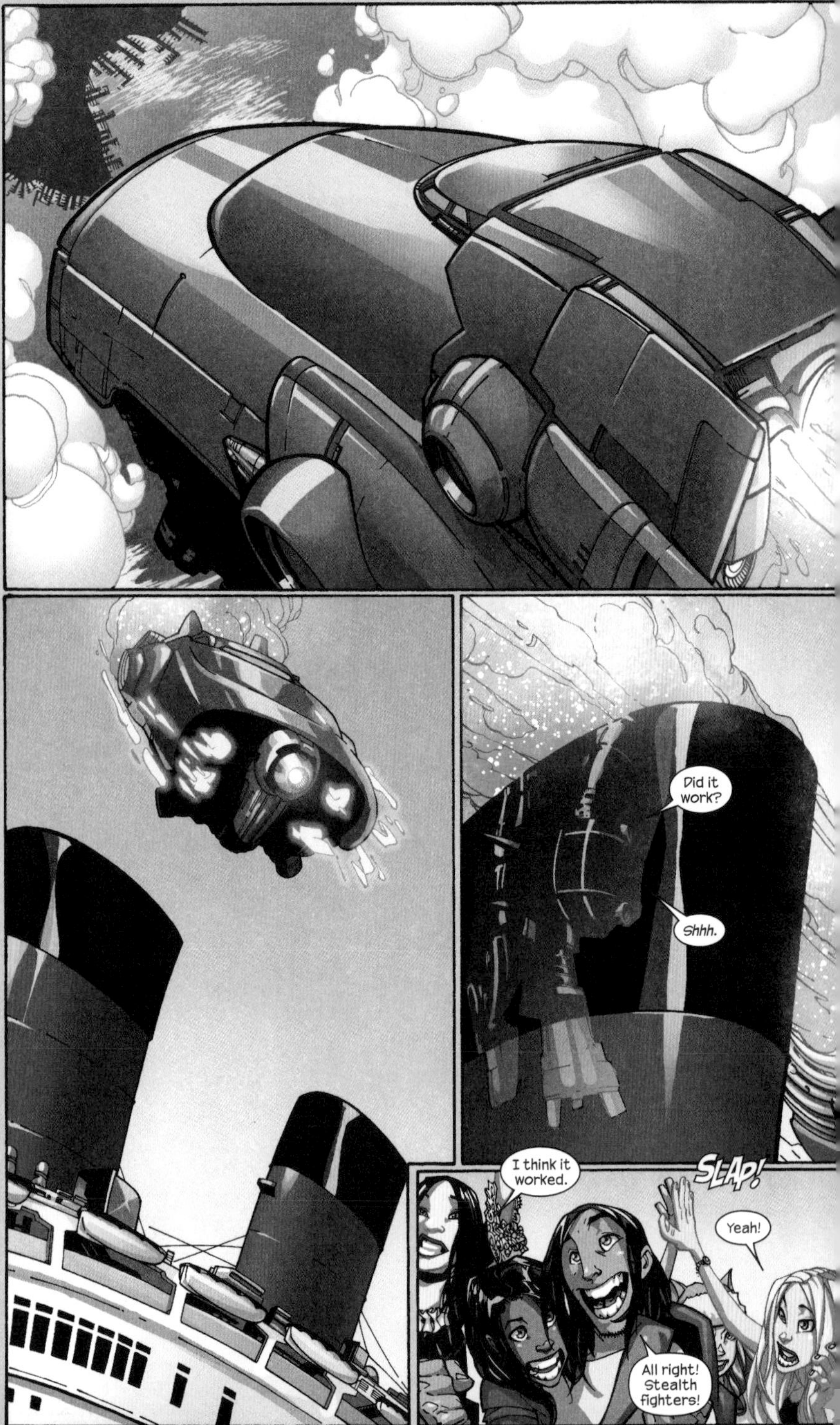
Did it work?
Shhh.
I think it worked.
SLAP!
Yeah!
All right! Stealth fighters!

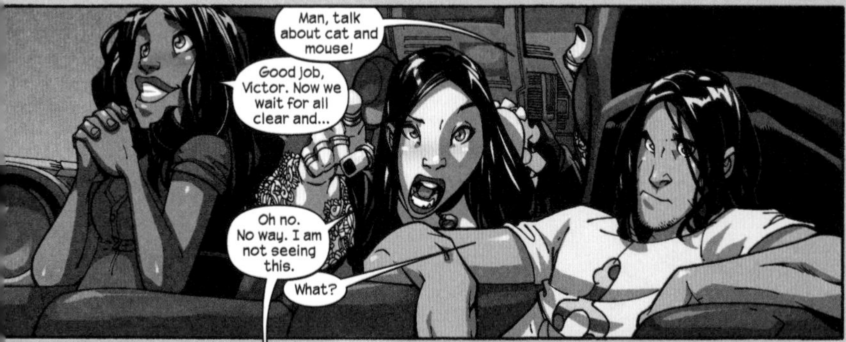
Man, talk about cat and mouse!
Good job, Victor. Now we wait for all clear and...
Oh no. No way. I am not seeing this.
What?

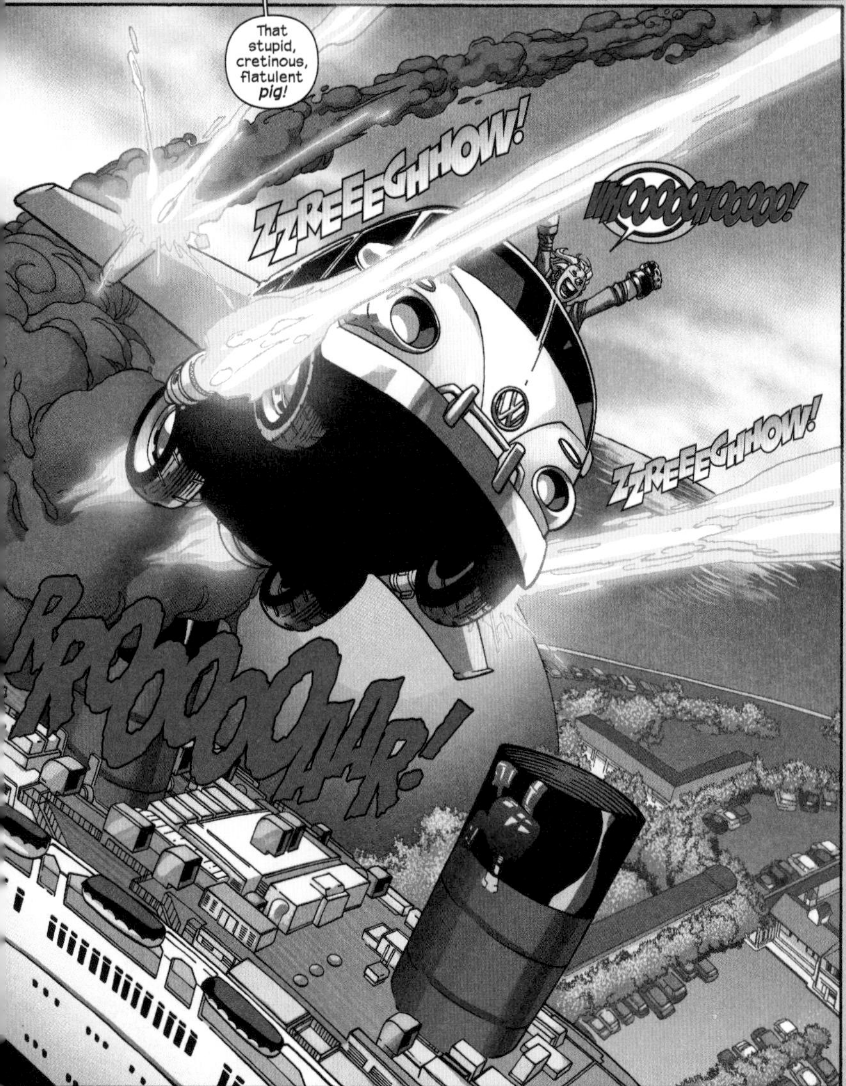
That stupid, cretinous, flatulent *pig!*
ZZREEEGHHOW!
WHOOOOOHOOOOO!
ZZREEEGHHOW!
RROOOOOAR!

6

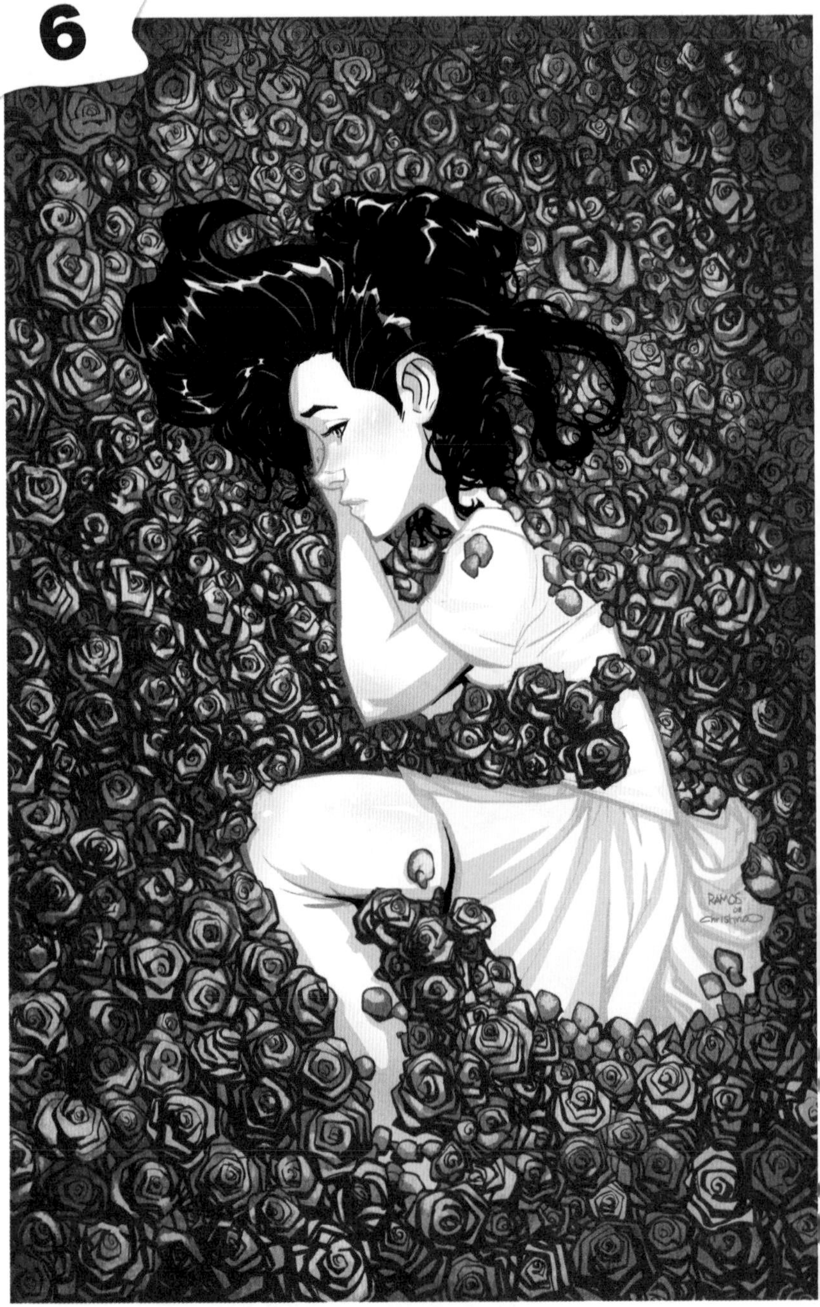
RAMOS

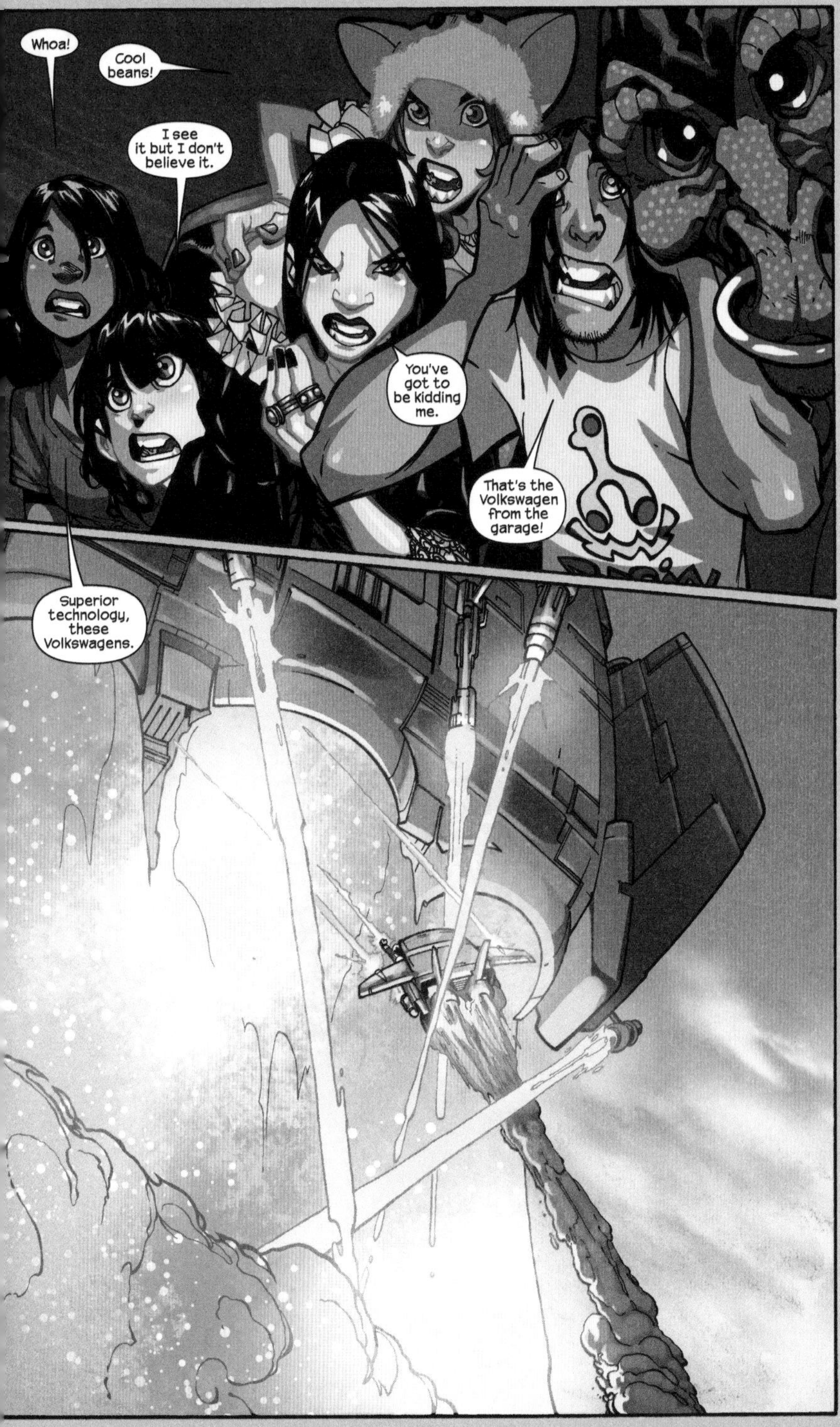
Whoa!
Cool beans!
I see it but I don't believe it.
You've got to be kidding me.
That's the Volkswagen from the garage!
Superior technology, these Volkswagens.

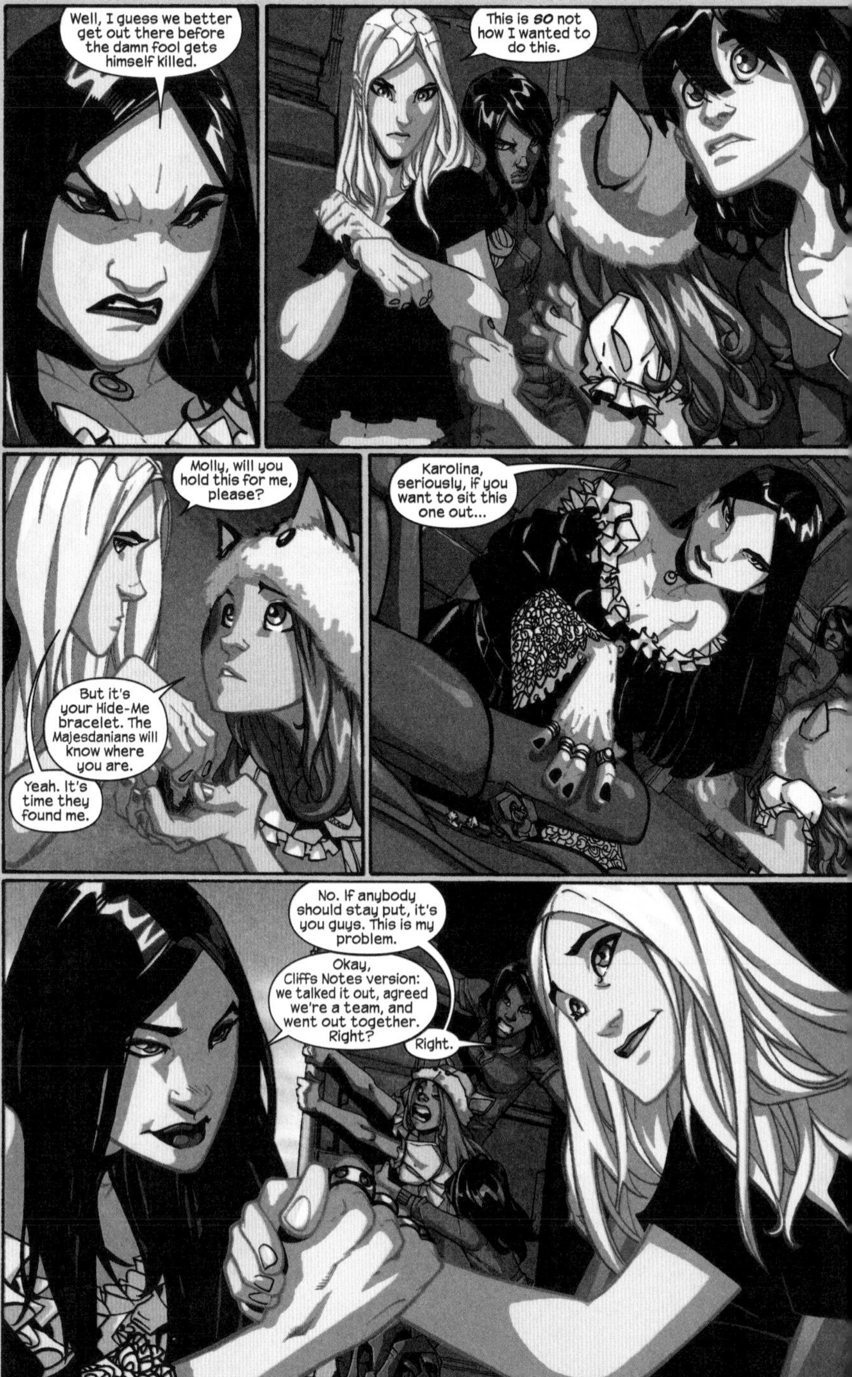
Well, I guess we better get out there before the damn fool gets himself killed.
This is SO not how I wanted to do this.
Molly, will you hold this for me, please?
But it's your Hide-Me bracelet. The Majesdanians will know where you are.
Yeah. It's time they found me.
Karolina, seriously, if you want to sit this one out...
No. If anybody should stay put, it's you guys. This is my problem.
Okay, Cliffs Notes version: we talked it out, agreed we're a team, and went out together. Right?
Right.

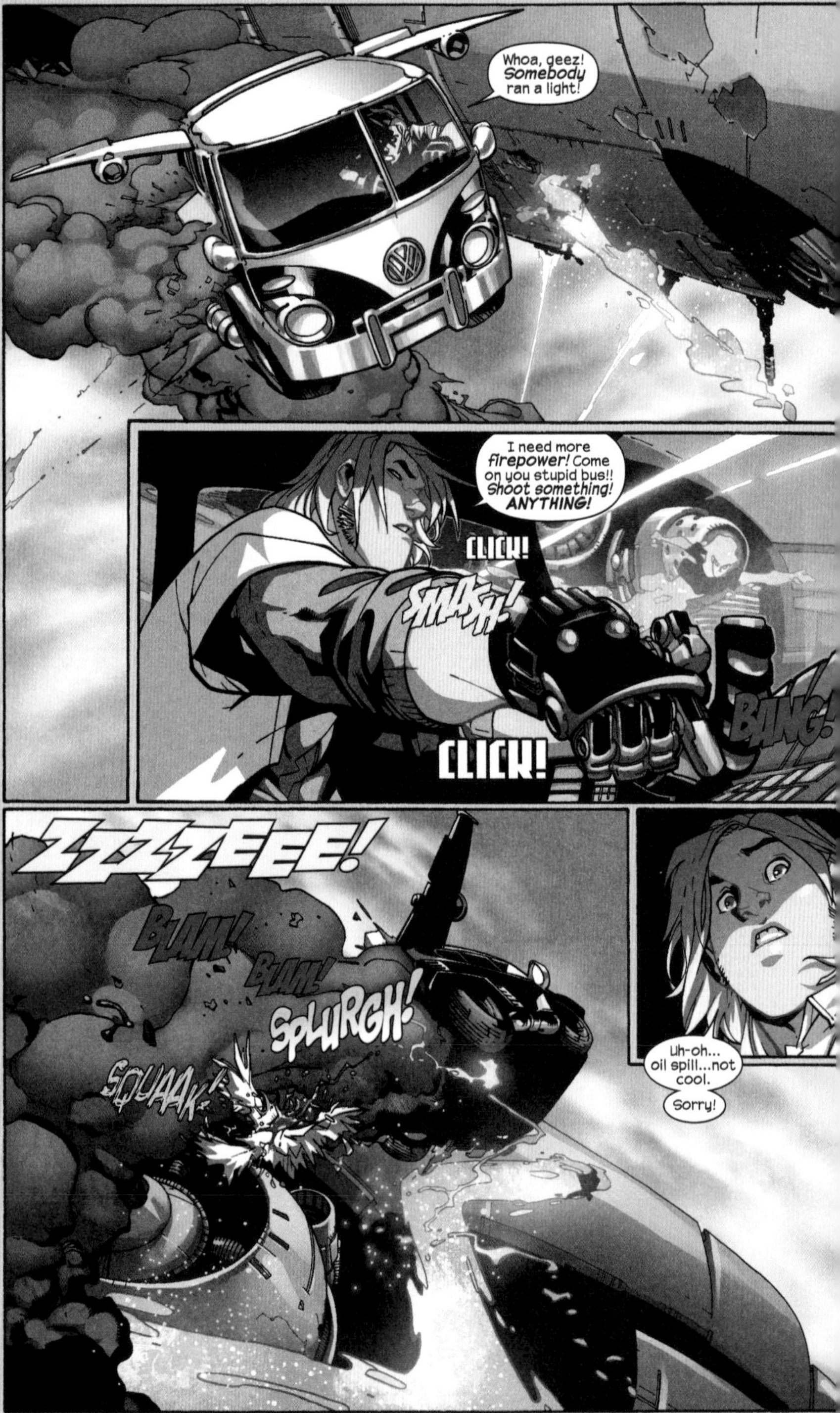

Whoa, geez! Somebody ran a light!
I need more firepower! Come on you stupid bus!! Shoot something! ANYTHING!
CLICK!
SMASH!
CLICK!
BANG!
ZZZZEEEE!
BLAM!
BLAM!
SPLURGH!
SQUAAK!
Uh-oh... oil spill...not cool.
Sorry!

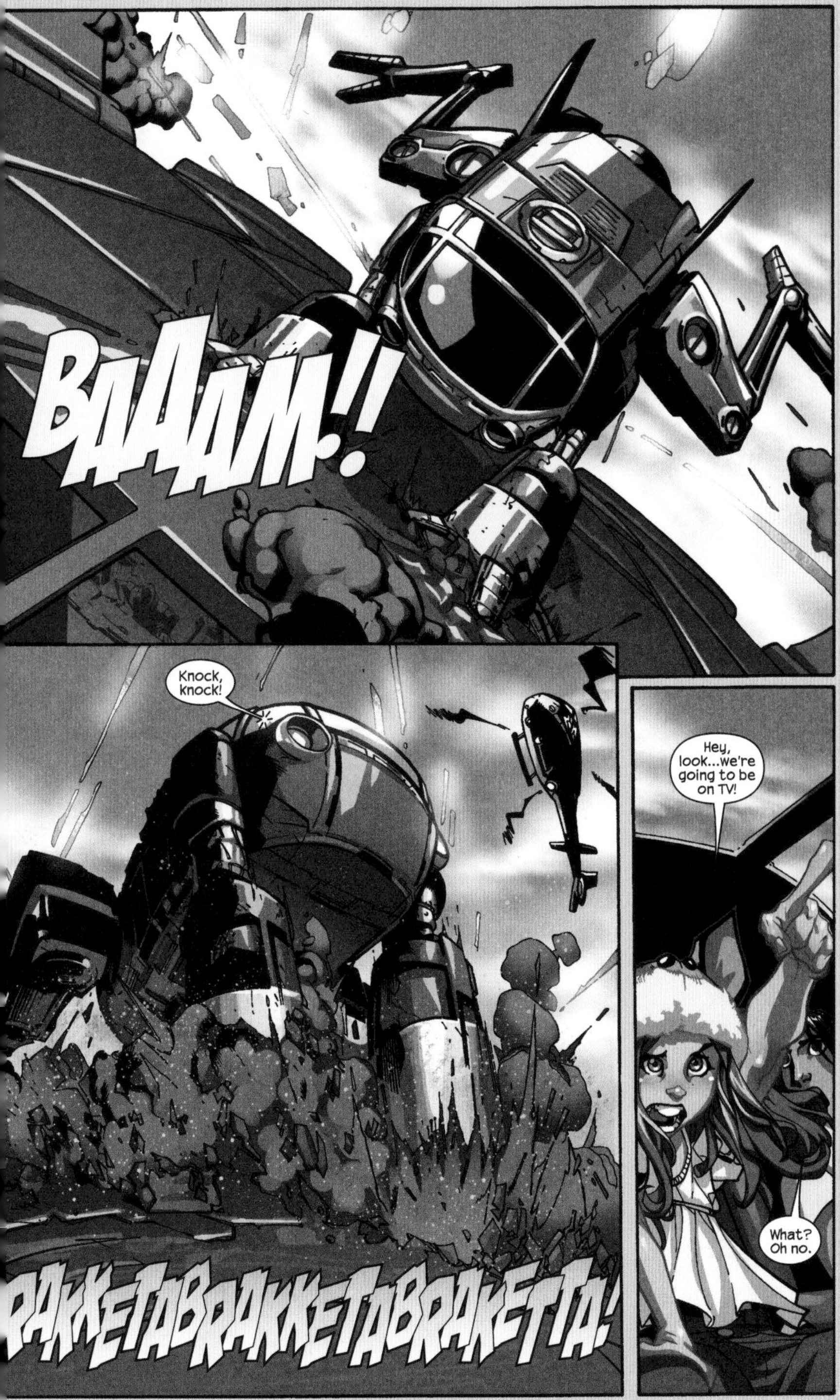
BAAAM!!
Knock, knock!
RAKKETABRAKKETABRAKETTA!
Hey, look...we're going to be on TV!
What? Oh no.

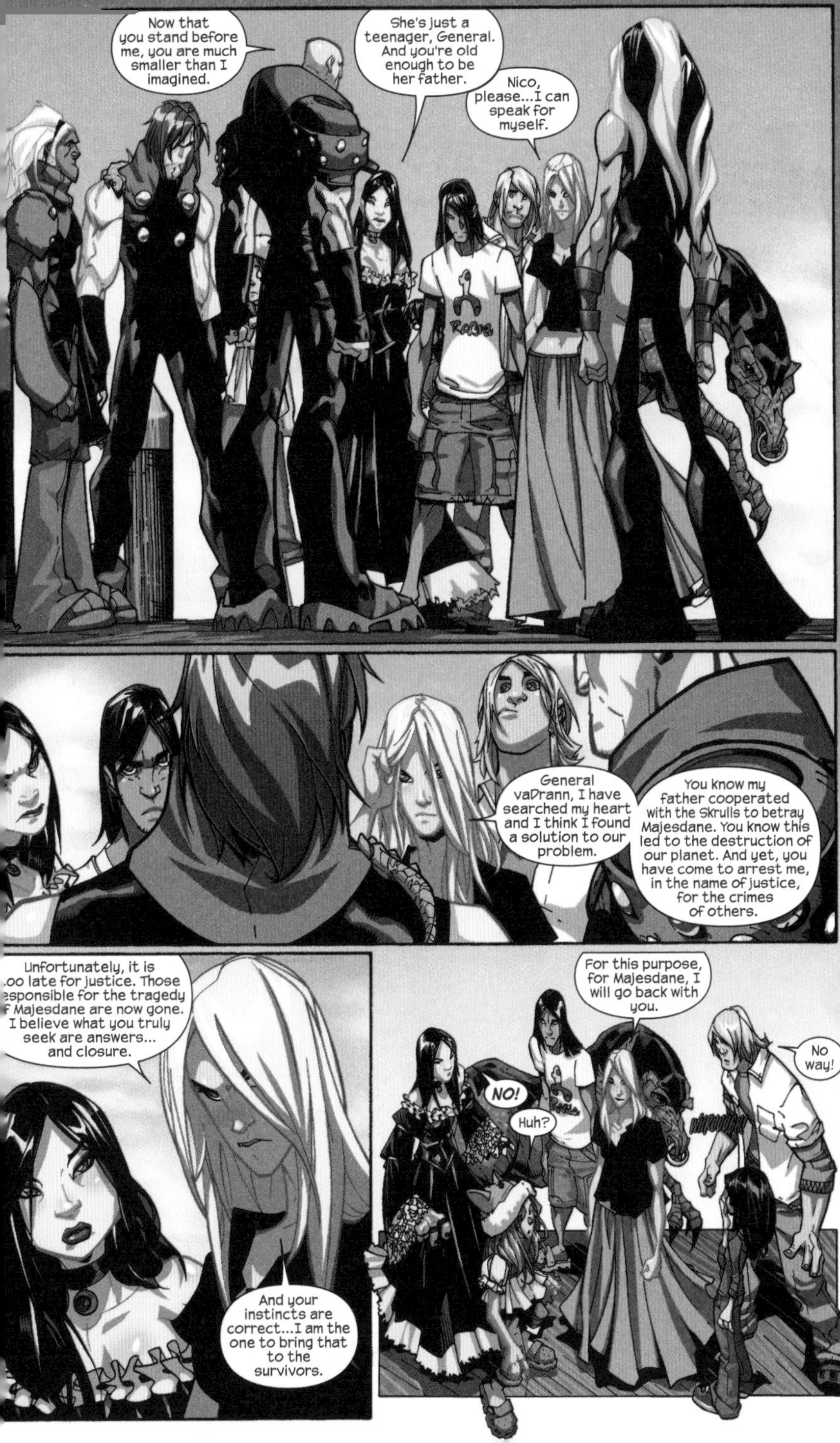
Now that you stand before me, you are much smaller than I imagined.
She's just a teenager, General. And you're old enough to be her father.
Nico, please...I can speak for myself.
General vaDrann, I have searched my heart and I think I found a solution to our problem.
You know my father cooperated with the Skrulls to betray Majesdane. You know this led to the destruction of our planet. And yet, you have come to arrest me, in the name of justice, for the crimes of others.
Unfortunately, it is oo late for justice. Those esponsible for the tragedy f Majesdane are now gone. I believe what you truly seek are answers... and closure.
And your instincts are correct...I am the one to bring that to the survivors.
For this purpose, for Majesdane, I will go back with you.
NO!
Huh?
No way!

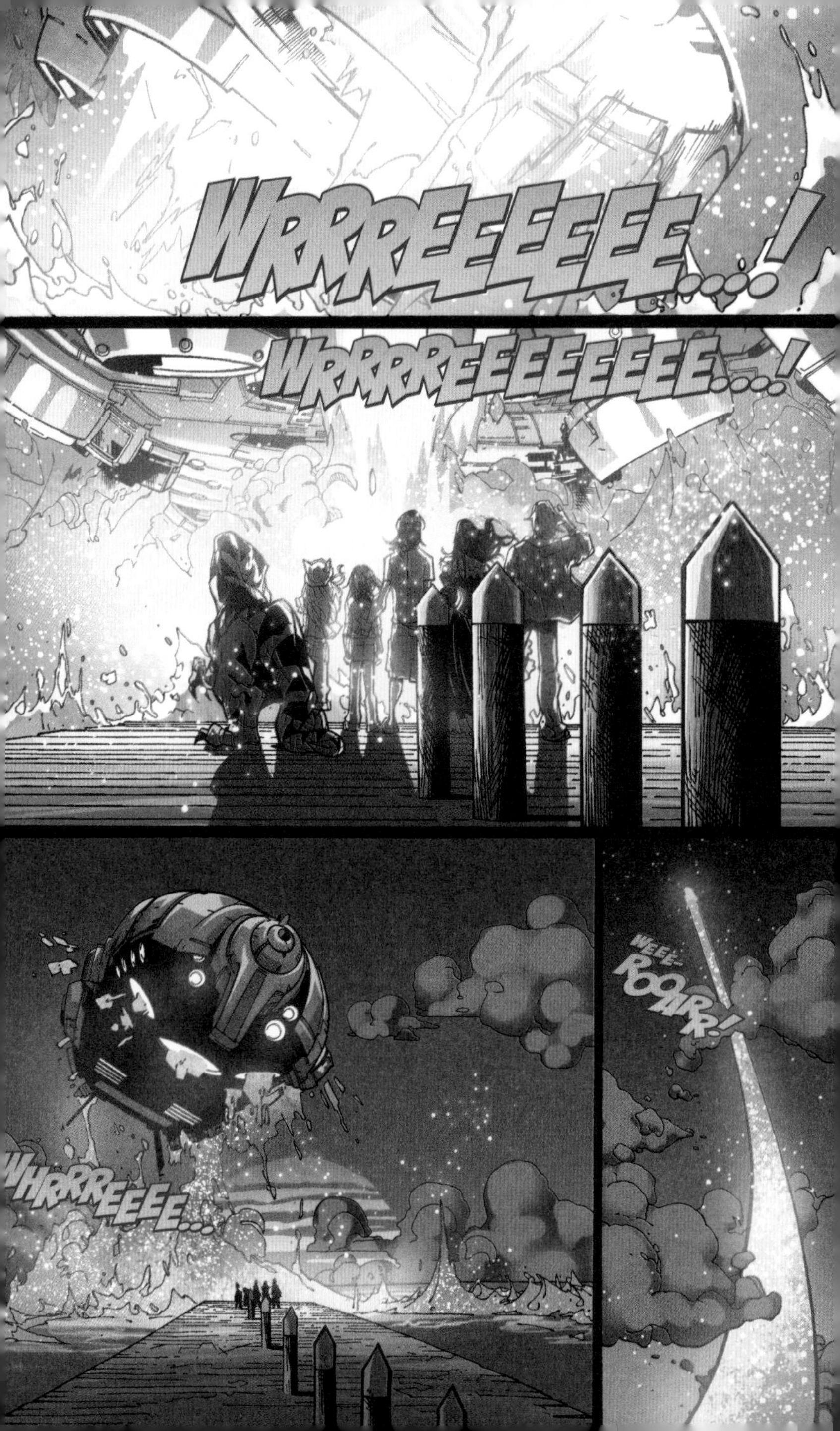
WRRREEEEEEE...!
WRRRRREEEEEEEE...!
WHRRRREEEE...
WEEE-ROOARR!

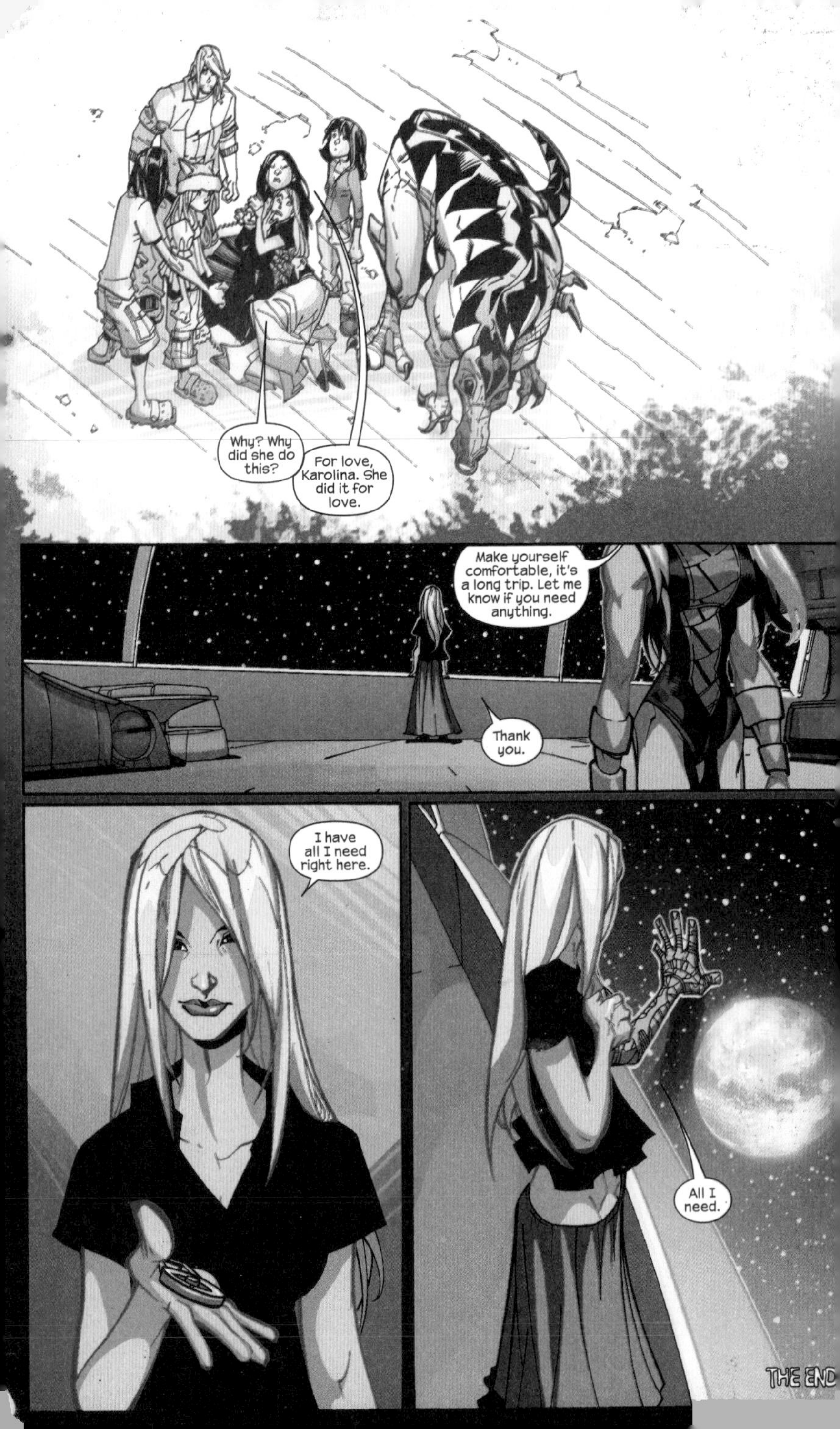

Why? Why did she do this?
For love, Karolina. She did it for love.
Make yourself comfortable, it's a long trip. Let me know if you need anything.
Thank you.
I have all I need right here.
All I need.
THE END